D0627407

Letters to Pope Francis

Rebuilding a Church with Justice and Compassion

Matthew Fox

Copyright © 2013 Matthew Fox

All rights reserved.

ISBN: 1490372970
ISBN-13:9781490372976

DEDICATION

To Sister Dorothy Stang, who was
my student and my teacher, and to
Oscar Romero and other martyrs
of the Americas whose sacrifices
and living of the Gospel call
church and society to reform and
renewal.

.

CONTENTS

Introductory Letter: The Promise of Your Namesake   7
for a Church on the Brink

1   Moving from a Schismatic Church to a Truly Catholic   14
    One

2   Why Religion is in Decline: Wisdom from Rabbi   31
    Heschel

3   Francis, the Cosmic Christ and the Future of Our   42
    Species

4   Francis, Youth, and Recovering Intergenerational   53
    Wisdom

5   Some Content for the New Evangelization and   74
    Revisioning the Sacrament of Ordination and
    Priesthood

6   Small Communities   94

7   The Sacrament of Liberation   117

8   Twelve Steps to Rebuilding the Church   128

    Bibliography   147

INTRODUCTORY LETTER: THE PROMISE OF YOUR NAMESAKE FOR A CHURCH ON THE BRINK

Dear Pope Francis:

We are brothers. We are both of the new world, you in South America, me in North America. We are the same generation—you are a few years older but we are both in our 70's—and as elders we are surely asking: "What can we leave behind that is worthwhile for future generations to live by?"

This is a precarious time to be a young person as so much health and beauty are disappearing from our Earth and the promise of economic success is diminishing for many amidst great global uncertainty. As you gather to celebrate the youth of the world in Rio around World Youth Day, I hope this letter assists your preparations. I am moved by the following poem by a rap artist who lives in my home state of California and its insistent challenge to live lives of conscience, awareness and service so that we might cut through denial and respond to the severe crises of our time. I am sure you agree with its urgency and exhortation:

it's 3:23 in the morning and I'm awake
because my great great grandchildren won't let me sleep
my great great grandchildren ask me in dreams
what did you go while the planet was plundered? what did
you do when the earth was unraveling?

surely you did something
when the seasons stared failing?
as the mammals, reptiles, birds were all dying? did you fill
the streets with protest
when democracy was stolen?

what did you do once
you knew?[1]

Pope Francis, we are both priests—I, though younger, was ordained a year or two before you. I think that means we both care about people and our task is to serve them even as they bless us. I liked how, when you were just elected Pope, you introduced yourself as "Bishop of Rome" and you asked the people first for their blessing and bowed toward them before you offered one from yourself.

You are a Jesuit and I was a Dominican for 34 years. Of course, our different traditions have had their scrapes and squabbles over the years, but none that mutual respect and fraternal rapprochement could not resolve. We share fraternal respect and admiration. As teachers and theologians, contemplatives in action, and as missionaries

---

[1] Drew Dellinger, "hieroglyphic stairway" in Drew Dellinger, *Love Letter to the Milky Way* (Ashland, Oregon, White Cloud Press: 2011).

in the Americas and Asia, we both no doubt like to brag about the exploits of our brothers be they Thomas Aquinas, Meister Eckhart, da Las Casas, Yves Congar, M.D. Chenu, Roland de Vaux or Edward Schillebeeckx in my camp or Francis Xavier, Pere Marquette, the Iroquois martyrs, Karl Rahner, Teilhard de Chardin, Anthony de Mello in yours.

And then there are our founders, so different in life experience and character and in the historic time they lived and worked—Dominic of Guzman (13th century) and Ignatius of Loyola (16th century), both of whom sought to render the church "useful" (to use Saint Hildegard of Bingen's word) in times of change and tumult in their day, so launched reform movements that have lasted even to today. My brother, Dominic, of course, was a contemporary and peer of your namesake, St. Francis.

So let us talk now about your chosen name, Francis. Yours was a daring choice and I hope that is a sign of a daring papacy to come since much courage is required of us elders at this crucial moment in human and planetary history.

Your choosing the name 'Francis' is daring in at least two regards. First, as you are fully aware, in the 800 years since Francis died no pope has ever dared to take his name. No doubt this is partly due to reverence for his unique brand of holiness and his iconic saintliness, but partly too I suspect because Francis was not a huge fan of the papacy, or indeed any kind of hierarchy. Francis wanted his band of brothers (and sisters) to remain that way always—a brotherhood—so as not to become an isolated clerical caste or hierarchical order.

Alas! His wishes were not granted (and his sisters were taken off the preaching circuit and locked up in monasteries), but at least his vision for a horizontal and circular fellowship (and sisterhood)—versus a ladder-like one—lives on in our minds and hearts.

Surely your choosing his name reveals your own preference for this vision of brotherhoods and sisterhoods, of bands and circles of people, rather than hierarchical ladder climbing. The implications of this choice for church reform are immense, as you well know. I take this to be the primary reason you dared to choose the name 'Francis' at this time of the dark night of the church. And dare you did!

There are those even now who criticize you and ask your motives in daring to undo 800 years of precedent, years of "hands-off" respect for Francis' name by popes. The complaints I have heard come from good people, Francis-lovers trying to live his values, who don't want his name sullied by politics, ecclesial or otherwise—and they wish you well, just the same. Will your breakthrough in choosing this revered name prove to be decisive for church renewal? We hope and pray and await your decision-making as both Pope and, as you say, Bishop of Rome.

Which brings us to the second dimension of daring in your name choice. We all know what a pioneer Francis was, how he broke with his father and with both the old feudalism and the new capitalism of his day, the latter of which his father actually spearheaded as a very successful businessman. And so we ask: Will you too break with the fathers of Wall Street and titans of power who espouse an oligarchy of wealth and power to dominate others by means of economic and political injustice the world over? Those who are hiding thirty-two trillion dollars in secret off-shore accounts to guarantee they and their corporations pay no income taxes to support the common good?[2] Will you stand for what and for whom Francis did when he stood up to wealth for wealth's sake in his day? We hope and pray that you will stand with "the Least" (Matthew 25) as Francis did and inspires you to do.

This will not be an easy task. The powerful do not relinquish their power happily as Mahatma Gandhi, Martin Luther King Jr. and Nelson Mandela observed. The powerful include giants of the media, oil, finance, food, weapons manufacturers and even government. We want to stand with you in courage in resisting efforts of the media to inflate ecclesial or papal egos to serve these gods of mammon.

Surely another reason for you choosing the name 'Francis' is that you feel, as so many of us do today, the urgency of the environmental catastrophe that awaits the whole planet—climate change, the destruction of species at untold numbers, the "greatest mass extinction spasm in 65 million years" as one scientist put it. Putting the weight of the papacy behind all efforts to defend imperiled nature would surely be a Francis-like approach to survival of the planet as we know it. Your choice to take public transportation to work and your rejection of papal limousines are fine gestures—personal modesty and environmental care do indeed go hand in hand—in the right direction. As a renowned scientist at Stanford University told me one day, "we are the first species in the 4.5 billion year history of this planet that can choose not to go extinct. But," he added, "we haven't made that choice yet." Surely your witness can help us—as individuals, governments and businesses need to make that choice.

---

[2] David Leigh, "Leaks reveal secrets of the rich who hide cash offshore," *The Guardian*, April 3, 2013.

Still another gift from Francis to our times is his amazing consciousness of gender balance. His poetry and his actions reveal a man who recognizes the necessary balance of masculine and feminine, yang and yin, in all beings and in all relationships if we are to be a sustainable species.

And finally, there is another reason we are all hoping you chose the name 'Francis.' It is that you would thereby be committed to performing his first vocation which was revealed to him by Christ: "to rebuild my church." From the bottom up the church is in desperate need of rebuilding and reforming (semper ecclesia reformanda). Every one everywhere seems to recognize this, except for the entrenched bureaucracy in the Vatican whose lust for power seems to extend everywhere and in every direction—power over the appointments of bishops and cardinals the world over, over liturgy, over thinkers, over women religious, over women hearing a call to ordination, over homosexuals, over married couples (forbidding birth control), over the divorced, over those with AIDS and contagious diseases (forbidding of condoms), over the young seeking new forms of worship, over the unmarried (no sex before marriage), and indeed over victims of pedophile priests.

You have set the bar very high in choosing the name Francis and being the first pope ever to dare to do so. Many of us want to support you in this ambitious choice of patrons and defend you from those who would wish to keep the Curia unreformed. We wish you well and God speed. I appreciate your willingness to listen to me, a simple brother and theologian, as I discuss with you in the letters that follow some thoughts about your new vocation as Bishop of Rome and the great good you can accomplish in that office.

You may be familiar with the American indigenous teaching that when the condor and the eagle fly together, peace will prevail. I hope that by the various histories we represent, I, who come from the North and land of the eagle, and you who come from the South and the land of the condor, may in these letters contribute to a rebirth of peace and the justice that upholds it.

1 MOVING FROM A SCHISMATIC CHURCH TO A TRULY CATHOLIC ONE

Dear Pope Francis:

In a recent book I made the point, citing a personal conversation with my late and esteemed Dominican brother, Father Schillebeeckx, that the Church of the past two papacies has been in schism. Beyond the fact as Schillebeeckx noted that "many European theologians agree" with his assessment, why do I say schism? Because, quite simply, in Catholic theology a Council trumps a Pope but a Pope does not trump a Council. This was the case in the fourteenth century when the Council of Constance, fed up with three popes vying for power over a forty-two year period, fired all three and hired a new one. Beginning with the reign of Pope John Paul II we have had two papacies mired in schism because they have been undoing the reforms and teachings of Vatican II, centralizing everything in the Curia, and thereby turning their back on a valid Council. Two papacies in schism.

By proceeding in schism, the absolute power amassed

by the Curia has produced absolute scandals just as the historian Lord Acton predicted over 120 years ago: "power corrupts and absolute power corrupts absolutely." The question now becomes, what are you going to do about this sordid snake pit of sexual, intellectual, financial and spiritual waywardness? Pope John Paul I attempted to clean up this mess, but his life was cut short.

Will you, in cleaning up these raging scandals, return to the principles and intentions of Vatican II whose fiftieth anniversary we just honored? Will you put an end to the New Inquisition waged by the Curial bureaucracy and its "third rate theologians" (my master general's phrase) over the past thirty-five years, which sought to turn back the clock on Vatican II's promised freedom of conscience and open debate among theologians? Surely, as a Jesuit coming from a proud tradition of educational excellence and intellectual endeavor, you must feel deeply for all those theologians to date who have been hounded, hunted, disbarred, expelled, deprived of their livelihoods, maliciously misrepresented, lied about, and chased by religious zealots. I am just one of those banished theologians but there have been at least 104 others from all around the world whom I name in my book, *The Pope's War: Why Ratzinger's Secret Crusade Has Imperiled the Church and How It Can Be Saved.* Surely you recognize the crying need in times as confusing and complex as ours—for intellectual debates and discussion, scholarship and questioning, on so many topics. Let us finally close down this Inquisition once and for all—just as Vatican II promised.

Just as General Motors can't run without engineers, neither can a religious tradition operate without theologians studying and debating. A professor of my alma mater, the Institut Catholique de Paris, which traces its roots to the first University in Paris where Aquinas and

Eckhart both taught, said to me several years ago when she heard me in dialogue with a scientist in the city of Chicago, "The Pope (John Paul II) and Cardinal Ratzinger have killed all theology in Europe. Theology is dead there. Nothing like what you did tonight could be happening in Europe." Maybe this is a principal reason why the European churches are as empty as they are—no thought allowed.

Your late brother Jesuit, Cardinal Mantini of Milan, wrote in his final will and testament that the Roman Catholic Church was "200 years behind the times." Vatican II sought to change history but its efforts have been for the most part voided.

Please do not be deceived by cheering crowds in St Peter's Square and adulatory media fawning over the papal theater that is the Vatican today; just as with British Royal and celebrity scandals their attention is driven by the need to keep up their ratings and revenues. The Vatican today is the last reigning monarchy on earth (though unlike other monarchies it doesn't allow women to rule or even to advise). Most people aren't really paying attention and most wonder—as Francis did in his day—what all the media-driven papalolatry has to do with preaching Gospel values of justice and compassion and with empowering the poor to stand up to the powers that be and assisting them to find their true voice. Your job too, is to empower the voiceless.

To liberate creation is to protect creation from human destruction. Recently I saw a photo of a large white shark in the water with a man in wet suit and diving gear near him and a caption read: "See the most dangerous being on the planet who will kill many….and next to him is a giant white shark." This is true. It is humans who are doing the greatest damage to our environment and to the many species that are going extinct today. Thomas Aquinas put it best 700 years ago, "one human being can do more evil than all the other species put together." So it is. Can we pull out of our denial and our narcissism as a species to change our ways radically so that other species may survive and our grandchildren can thrive? Can religion be part of the solution and not the problem? How might a pope imbued with the values of St. Francis contribute to such a meaningful and hopeful shift?

First, we need to listen to the people whom the Second Vatican Council rightly defined as "the church." Hierarchy exists to serve the people and not the other way around. St. John Henry Newman also famously remarked that if forced to choose between the pope and his conscience he would drink to conscience every time. Moreover, he observed, the church would look funny indeed without the laity. The laity are the *sensus fidelium*, the sense of the faithful. What they think and intuit matters, as the great Council affirmed. So let us once again have a church that listens and hears them out. To understand more fully what people are thinking, I propose we look closely at the foremost issues on the minds of those who consider the Church schismatic:

1. Sex. An early twentieth century Celtic poet wrote a poem called "Pater Noster" in which he compares the Church to a great sailing vessel that survived over centuries through typhoon and hurricanes, great waves and high seas, schisms and corruption. In the twentieth century it came up against giant rocks, crashed, splintered and sank. The name of the rocks was: Sex.

Yes, the Church dances with oblivion as it makes pronouncements on the subject of sex while ignoring the *sensus fidelium*, as well as contemporary science. Even worse, its relentless focus of more rules and commandments precludes authentic teaching and practice of the mysticism of sexuality, bearing witness to the divine encounter that ecstasy and love-making include. The Church's preoccupation with pelvic morality is a scandal in itself. Did Jesus occupy himself with such issues? It is a sign of a dysfunctional, and indeed developmentally frozen, consciousness. The late and wonderful Benedictine monk, Fr. Bede Griffiths, who lived in an ashram in India for over fifty years, has said that "if Christianity cannot recover its mystical tradition and teach it, it should just fold up and go out of business. It has nothing to offer." Instead of teaching the reality and practice of sexual mysticism, of love, love-making and tasting the Divine, the Church has chosen to preach endlessly about rules and regulations around sex. Moralizing is a weak substitute for mysticism. It makes one wonder whether we worship a God of Life or a God of Religion.

I sense that we are on the same page in this matter when I read your words: "We speak of morals because it is easier. Furthermore—and this is bad taste—we deal with themes related to matrimonial morals and those tied to the sixth commandment because they seem more colorful. Thus we give a very sad image of the Church." (1.60)

Consider the following realities:

About Birth Control

Over ninety percent of catholic women are practicing birth control. Many priests of my generation quit the priesthood because they could not in good conscience teach couples not to practice birth control in an age of excessive human population and not to use condoms in an age of AIDS and other serious transmittable diseases. Tragically, the "Humane Vitae" encyclical (1968) has become a litmus test for Catholic orthodoxy, serving for the past 45 years as a grotesque political bludgeon to disfigure and mute the face of the *sensus fidelium*. I appreciate your observation when you spoke of "anti-condom zealots" who want to "stick the whole world inside a condom." (1.10)

About Pre-marital Sex

Today with many young adults putting off marriage until they are twenty nine or so, it is foolish to teach that sex is for married couples only. Are we teaching that young people are to be celibate virgins for 14 years (say, from 15 years old to 29 years old)? That is silly. It scraps the Church's relevance for the young and divorces it from what it should be offering which is teachings of how sexual love is a mystical experience and ecstasy carries its own responsibilities. Scholars for the most part agree that Jesus' parents were probably not married at the time of his birth, and Jesus spent very little time preoccupied with such matters himself. One reason young adults today can't hear the Church is that it is out of tune with their as well as their caring parents' *sensus fidelium*. The arts of love and responsible friendship and love-making and mystical encounter is something that young people need to learn.

About Homosexuality

There is no question that homosexuality is the Galileo case of our twenty-first century. Just as in the 17th century the Church insisted it knew the sun moved about the earth and refused to listen to science, so today the Church refuses to listen to science which informs us that 8 to 10% of any human population is going to be gay or lesbian and that at least 484 other species include gay and lesbian populations. Thus homosexuality is not an "unnatural" minority. In the United States today 83% of young adults favor gay marriage. The case is closed. The *sensus fidelium* has spoken.

In arguing against abortion you invoke science saying that the genetic code is present from the start and you conclude: "It's not, therefore, a religious question but clearly a moral one, based on science."[3] Surely the same argument pertains to homosexuality. It is not a religious question but a scientific one and science has spoken. Have you ever known gay couples? Eaten in their homes and listened to their stories? Perhaps heard from some of their parents who may have had to learn along the way like you need to do? Why should a homosexual have to live a life of celibacy? My Bible says "God is love"—not that "God is heterosexual love only." If marriage and commitment is a value to a society, why would the Church not want to support committed gay couples as well as committed heterosexual couples? Invoking the Book of Leviticus against gays does not cut the mustard since the same book also calls eating shrimp an "abomination," teaches that stoning people to death for adultery is okay and endorses slavery. Among indigenous peoples in the Americas, Africa, Ireland and elsewhere it is well known that "two-spirited" peoples carry special spiritual depth to the community. This is why the spiritual directors to most Indian chiefs in America were homosexual. A homophobic religion deprives itself of spiritual depth.

About Abortion

For the past twenty five years, people attending my lectures have frequently asked for my position on abortion. My response consistently elicits applause. We should always be conservative about anything as precious and

---

[3] Michael Warren, "Pope Francis, in his own words, on the issues," *Yahoo! News*, April 22, 2013, http://news.yahoo.com/pope-francis-own-words-issues-163630499.html.

mysterious as human life of which even the most learned among us still carry so much ignorance. You cannot legislate good morality—this is an axiom in any introductory course on ethics. While I am against abortion on principle, I am not against people who make the morally tough decision to have an abortion. And I am even more against politicians (of all people!) telling women what to do with their bodies especially in tragic criminal instances of rape or incest.

With the exception of China, I do not know of a law anyplace else, that forces a woman to have an abortion. The law in my country and others where it is legal only allows that if one is to have an abortion (and abortion is an old practice in all cultures past and present), it is right to make it as safe and clean as possible to inflict minimal harm. I have never known a woman who found abortion to be an easy moral decision, but in some cases, such as rape, it seemed like the better choice.

Let us not condemn those who have abortions or those who pass laws safeguarding the bodies of women who feel they must have an abortion and have their physicians' support to do so. Great theologians of the past including Thomas Aquinas and Hildegard of Bingen pronounced on abortion in a very different manner from those know-it-all zealots who are shouting so loudly in the name of religion today. The fetus is not ready for the powerful human soul, they said, until several months into its maturation; before then the fetus starts out as a vegetable, then becomes an animal and only in a later stage does it become fully human.

It is materialistic modern science that has presumed there is no special gift of a human soul. This is not what the theological tradition has taught, at least until very recently, and I for one have never seen the scientific or theological argument to support it. In place of an argument supported theologically or scientifically, opponents of abortion have launched a politically charged one, insinuating (though not always in so many words) that women must not have control over their bodies and that only the father or an all-male hierarchy knows best. That a political domination of women drives much of the rhetoric against abortion cannot be denied.

Finally, Thomas Aquinas reminds us that "a mistake about creation results in a mistake about God." Thus in these areas of sexuality, old shibboleths (such as "homosexuality is unnatural") need to be replaced by science. Such shibboleths are mistakes about creation. They have resulted therefore in mistakes about God that have been mined as fodder by religious zealots and religious guarantors of their own prideful positions of power in a blind and nameless ecclesial bureaucracy known as the Curia. Back in the twelfth century, Saint Hildegard of Bingen referred to them in a letter to the pope as "hens who cackle in the night scaring even themselves." (11.103) Not much has changed.

When it comes to sexuality, the Church has not been teaching the message of Jesus about love and the nearness of the kingdom of God. Instead, it relies on a strangely narrow teaching derived from Augustine of Hippo that all human sexuality must be justified and legitimized by having children. It is because of Augustine and not Jesus that the Church finds itself forbidding birth control in a time of excessive human population explosion, condoms in an age of AIDS, premarital sex when marriage is being postponed and takes place much later than in the age of much shorter life span, and homosexuality when we now know it is a universal though minority condition. It is time to put a better theology together with science and some common sense, the *sensus fidelium.*

2.   Hypocrisy. I was pleased to see you speak out against ecclesial hypocrisy lately. I hope all the cardinals take your words to heart. Recently the cardinal of Scotland had to step down from his post and recuse himself from participating in the papal conclave because three priests had the courage to tell the truth that he had personally, as a bishop and as their boss, forced them to have sex with him on various occasions. This particular cardinal was the most vocal opponent of homosexual relations and marriage in the entire island of the UK. He was the poster boy for the anti-gay marriage forces, and harangued and huffed and puffed and preached and maneuvered to see that gays did not have the same rights as other Britons including the right to marry. The man is a homosexual. He is also an abuser in the work place as the priests testified that had they refused him their 'careers' in the clergy would have been seriously jeopardized because he was their 'boss.' According to legal statutes in Scotland and in my country which protect workers from the advances of sexually predatory supervisors, he belongs in jail.

While justice under the law eludes, another deeper problem remains for the Church—Hypocrisy. This is the real crime here. What kind of immoral men wear the cardinal red robes, wrapping themselves in lies by preaching while on the side abusing their power to satisfy their desires? This is at the core of what's behind the Vatican crises today; this is the story of how power corrupts. Corrupt and twisted cardinals, covering their crimes with even more corrupt preaching.

3.   Power. "Power corrupts and absolute power corrupts absolutely." These words from Lord Acton are more apt today than ever. The statement was made in response to the first Vatican Council (1869-1870) that declared the pope to be infallible. This doctrine has suffered from the temptations to appropriate all teaching,

appointments of bishops and decision-making to the confines of a centralized Vatican and away from the ecclesial life of national synods and lay-led parishes. It has led to squelching theological research, discussion and debate. The Second Vatican Council (1962-1965) sought to mitigate these errors, but over the last 35 years, two papacies have turned their back repeatedly on Vatican II in favor of a "galloping infallibility" that has amounted to nothing more than an ecclesial coup meant to diminish the contribution of lay leadership and embolden a harmful new Inquisition directed at theologians.

You speak out against a globalization that fails to respect cultural differences when you say: "The globalization that makes everything uniform is essentially imperialist...it is not human. In the end it is a way to enslave the nations." (1.158) I agree, but doesn't that apply to religion as well? Religion that fails to respect cultural and intellectual diversity is also imperialist and is used to subjugate.

What has been the result of all this Centralization? Corruption. Staggering, overwhelming corruption. Pope Benedict XVI received a report about call-boys blackmailing Curial hierarchy and all the facts will someday come to the light. Such a report is a natural outcome in an environment that fosters corruption, promoting the appointment of so-called leaders on the basis of their proclivity to act as Yes-men rather than being purveyors of conscience and justice. The appointment of these Yes-men has everything to do with the pedophile crisis and its horrendous cover-up to preserve the institution at all costs, even at the immeasurable cost to children. This corruption is further enabled by the dumbing down of the Church that stifles serious theological research and discussion, and infected with financial malfeasance of every kind that has given rise to fundraising sects of dubious moral standing such as Opus Dei, Communion and Liberation and the Legion of Christ, to places of prominence and power and decision-making in the Church worldwide.

Not only is your birthplace of the South American continent now flooded with Opus Dei hierarchy, but my North America is also feeling the same disease. On the West coast of the United States, where I live, the two most influential dioceses, Los Angeles and San Francisco, are now headed by Opus Dei archbishops (one of whom will be a cardinal someday). Both are young. They will reign for generations. Another Opus Dei bishop in America, Bishop Flynn of Kansas City has been convicted of hiding a pedophile priest by the civil court but he has refused to resign his position and apparently no one in the Vatican will hold him to account. The message from the Vatican has been unequivocal—no firing for hypocrisy, breaking the law, or covering up the most heinous of pedophile crimes. Only for speaking out about injustice to women (as was the case with two Australian bishops) do bishops get chastised and deposed.

Such are the sad and sordid fruits of Centralization that has dominated two papacies and has created a schism in the Church, or as a Catholic paper in India put it shortly before the papal conclave "a civil war in the Church." This is dramatic language and it comes from a non-dramatic Catholic scene, Catholics being a tiny and generally quiet minority in India. A civil war indeed. The Curia against the people. A Curia very happy to define itself as the Church contrary to the teachings of Vatican II and the authentic theological tradition as represented by Saint and Doctor of the Church, Hildegard of Bingen, who defines the Church as its people and especially the lay people and who teaches that the Logos is head of the Church and not the papal curia.

4. Lack of Spirituality. I know of a Native American woman, a Roman Catholic, who several years ago, under Pope John Paul II, attended a special beatification ceremony at the Vatican in honor of Blessed Tekewitha, a Mohawk woman who was recently canonized a saint. Never having been to Rome, she was looking forward to the special occasion. Sadly, she came back shaking her head and saying "there are evil spirits in that place." Coming from a modest woman of great depth, an elder of the church with her conscience and consciousness still intact, the pronouncement carried an ominous ring of truth. She never wanted to go near the Vatican again.

A friend of mine from Central America who is also indigenous had a similar experience at the Vatican a few years ago. He said: "I do not feel an ounce of spirituality in this place. Unlike Chartres Cathedral, for example, where I felt deeply the presence of the Black Madonna and more." Those with spiritual perception are not deceived by what has been going on in St. Peter's Square.

A young Catholic theologian in the United States named Jamie Manson has pointed out that when the priestly pedophile crisis broke out in the United States, today's young adults were ten years old—the exact age of the victims. No wonder they find it impossible to trust the church hierarchy. They have grown up with the awareness that the hierarchy essentially covered up for pedophile priests to preserve the "image" of the institution going out of their way often to do so, spending hundreds of millions of lay peoples' hard-earned money to hire lawyers to obfuscate the facts, forcing many victims into deeper depression, addictions, even suicide. One Cardinal, notorious for passing one priest who abused over 150 boys from parish to parish was actually promoted to important positions in Rome as head of the Santa Maria Maggiore basilica AND to the congregation of bishops helping to appoint new bishops around the world and specifically in the United States. I speak of course of Cardinal Law, who many feel should be in jail not in the red-robed splendor of Vatican largesse. And certainly not in a position where he is appointing bishops worldwide, denouncing Catholic sisters in America as he has done. There are many such shameful stories not only in the US but in Ireland, Belgium, Austria and Germany, as you well know.

Indeed, Cardinal Bertone, the secretary of state handpicked by Pope Benedict to run the Vatican wrote a deliriously cheerful preface to Father Maciel's book praising his "holiness" among other things even though the research into Maciel's notorious sexual abuse of twenty of his seminarians had already been known by the Congregation of the Doctrine of Faith which Ratzinger headed at the time. Indeed, Ratzinger was personally handed a letter by Bishop Carlos Talavera in June 1999 that detailed the truths around Maciel. (1a. pp.217ff) As all now know, Maciel, coddled by the Vatican for so long (including plane rides with the pope and special Masses in St Peter's square to ordain his priests), had two wives on the side and four children all of whom, boys and girls, he sexually abused. A fraud! Even his book, so praised by Bertone, was proven to be plagiarized from a priest who wrote much of it in 1943.[4] To this day Bertone has not apologized, and without apology he runs the very same machinery that made you Bishop of Rome.

No doubt you understand why it would be difficult for anyone with even a limited awareness of this corruption and hypocrisy to trust an organization like the one the Roman Catholic Church has become, especially when it

---

[4] Jason Berry, *Render Unto Rome: The Secret Life of Money in the Catholic Church* (New York: Crown Publishers, 2011), p. 284.

claims to speak in the name of Jesus himself. How much more corruption and hypocrisy has to be revealed before Catholics everywhere get their heads out of the sand, throw off denial, demand reformation or simply move on? One prominent lay Catholic historian, Garry Wills, has clearly had it with the papacy and hierarchy of our day. In a recent interview he called the papacy as "irrelevant" as the queen of England.[5] Most monarchies have moved on, but the Vatican and its absolutist monarchy seems to have dug in its heels and amassed all ecclesial power to its red-silked court and its curial courtiers, while the corruption piles higher and higher all around it for all to see and smell and taste.

Given these realities, why should we be surprised that only 10% of Catholics are practicing in your homeland of Argentina and fewer less in most European countries? When I was in Rome a year ago a local man in his early forties came up to me and said: "I used to call myself a Catholic. Now I just call myself a Christian." It is very telling that a man brought up in the city of Rome with all its ecclesial history can no longer identify with the schismatic Catholic Church that the Vatican has spawned. It seems that right under the pope's nose Catholics are abandoning a sinking ship. Yes, many have given up on the papacy as we know it. A number of years ago I was leading a retreat in upstate New York with about 150 people in attendance. I asked their religious affiliation. About 100 identified as Catholic. "How many of you are practicing?" I asked. About 60 raised their hands. "And how many of your children are practicing," I asked. No one raised a hand.

---

[5] Sally Quinn, "Garry Wills: Papacy Should Fade into Symbolic Irrelevance Like Queen Elizabeth," *Washington Post*, March 19, 2013.

No one.

Why should we be surprised at the response from a young and very caring adult who is doing saintly and prescient work with street youth in New York City (and previously did the same with youth in India), to my question of how to reform or save the church: "Save the church? There is nothing left to save. The only question is who gets the property." This man is not ignorant about Roman Catholicism. He grew up in Poland under the shadow of the Soviet regime and the dawn of the Solidarity revolution. He personally knew priests who were tortured and martyred by the Soviets. But he has no illusions that the Catholic Church as represented by Pope John Paul II or the last papacy has much to do with the Gospels or authentic teachings of Jesus. He is not alone. Many of his generation feel the same.

You have your hands full, Pope Francis, and I and many others wish you well. But clearly your task begins at home with a deep housecleaning in the Curia itself. Your rather rapid move in appointing an eight-person team chosen from many countries is indeed a promising first step in trying to restore this deformed institution. This has gone far beyond a matter of bringing law-breakers to true justice; it requires a re-education of a whole privileged caste of errant, arrogant, theologically-challenged souls who have put their own advancement ahead of the spirit of ministry.

Jesus was not silent about abuse of children, was he? He proposed that those who mistreat children be given a millstone around their necks and jump into the waters. ALL those who covered up priestly abuse should belong to the "millstone club" (OM, order of millstones) and should wear badges the shape of millstones until repentance is done and administered so that all will know whom not to trust. This must include cardinals and bishops for sure.

Is it any wonder that I hear theologians and priests in Latin America saying, "We used to serve the church; now we serve humanity." People are going beyond the church and outgrowing its structures everywhere. We need less of structures and more of the Gospel and its values of justice and compassion preached and lived.

Ours is a low time in church history that will be remembered as the Great Schism, a time that distanced the Church from both the Gospel and from Vatican II. Will your papacy be of another sort altogether? Will it commit to Francis' values and those of the Gospel? One prays and waits and watches. Meanwhile, the real church, that of the people, is at work, getting made and remade, being born and dying and born again in the creativity of the Spirit, producing works of grace and abundant imagination. One hopes the ecclesial powers can and will join it. But one cannot hold one's breath or wait around. There is too much work to do, too many endangered beings and humans calling out for succor and assistance as you well know.

2 WHY RELIGION IS IN DECLINE: WISDOM FROM RABBI HESCHEL

Dear Pope Francis:

I have taken note of the fact that you and Rabbi Abraham Skorka in Argentina have become good friends; he speaks highly of you to the press. I have enjoyed reading your dialogs with him and I commend you for learning and listening from him. This pleases me very much because as we both know anti-Semitism has haunted Christian history since its earliest days and it built up over the centuries, spurred on by the sixteenth century pope Paul IV who invented the ghetto for Jews in Rome. It became even more fierce and unchecked with the horrors of Hitler's crusade and fascism in general has always dined on that sordid, anti-Semitic legacy. As we both know, Jesus and his earliest followers were Jewish, so surely church renewal has something essential to do with embracing and celebrating a Jewish consciousness and with undoing our ignorance of, and what is sometimes contempt for, Jesus' lineage.

Recent scholarship on Pope Pius XI reveals how he asked a North American Jesuit, Father John LaFarge, who had written about racism in America, to draft an encyclical on the evil of fascism. Lafarge unfortunately sent his document first to his Superior General, Father Wlodimir Ledochowski, who it turns out held fascist sympathies and did not pass it on to the pope. Eventually he did release it but the whole process was slowed down and Pope Pius XI died the night before he was to deliver an anti-fascist speech and before he published his anti-fascist encyclical. (Cardinal Eugene Tisserant of France, who was the pope's best friend, wrote in his diary that the pope had been murdered.) The next pope, Pius XII, as we know, never wrote an encyclical condemning fascism. How much history might have been changed—how possible is it that Pius XI's encyclical might have prevented Hitler's and Mussolini's advances had it been promulgated—we will never know.[6]

I too have been blessed by knowing and working with rabbis including Rabbis Zalman Schachter (founder of the Jewish Renewal movement), Arthur Waskow, Michael Lerner (editor of Tikkun), Rami Shapiro, and others. But I especially want to invoke in this subject of religious renewal the brilliant spirit and solid analysis of Rabbi Abraham Joshua Heschel who wrote so many books of depth and beauty including the classic work, *The Prophets*. He not only composed that scholarly volume, he also lived it. He literally walked his talk when he marched with Martin Luther King at Selma to protest racism and segregation and he was vilified by his own Jewish community for doing so because they felt his public presence on behalf of black people would arouse still more

---

[6] Peter Eisner, "Pope Pius XI's Last Crusade," *Huffington Post Religion*, April 15, 2013.

anti-Semitism. He marched anyway and when his ten year old daughter asked him what it was like marching amidst the dangers at Selma he replied: "I felt my feet were praying."

I noticed that Rabbi Skorka cited Heschel in his dialogs with you and for good reason. Thus I feel emboldened to cite him about the all-important topic of when religion goes sour or sick. Heschel had this to say about religion in our time: "It is customary to blame secular science and anti-religious philosophy for the eclipse of religion in modern society. It would be more honest to blame religion for its own defeats. Religion declined not because it was refuted, but because it became irrelevant, dull, oppressive, insipid. When faith is completely replaced by creed, worship by discipline, love by habit; when faith becomes an heirloom rather than a living fountain; when religion speaks only in the name of authority rather than with the voice of compassion—its message becomes meaningless." (14.29) These wise and prophetic words on the demise of religion in our time speak very strongly to me.

He is so right—it is customary to blame secular science and anti-religious philosophy. So many essentially cynical religious apologists begin their theology with a loud dualism—the "secular" thinkers vs. themselves, though rarely defining what and whom they mean by secular. There are remnants of the "abhor the world" religion of 17th century France lurking in such grand dualisms along with a deep intellectual laziness. "We are the spiritual ones and those worldly ones ought to be damned." It is always dangerous to ground one's religion on dualisms—is God the Creator not also Creator of the whole world including the world humans create? There also lurks a dangerous element of righteousness in the "we are holding all the answers" component of such dualisms. It is such righteousness that opens the door to religious fanaticism.

"It would be more honest to blame religion for its own defeats." Yes, believers need to cease projecting onto imagined or real enemies their shortcomings and take a hard and critical look within. Self-criticism is part of any authentic spiritual (as opposed to mere ideological and projection-filled) spiritual journey. What has religion done or failed to do?

"Religion becomes irrelevant, dull, oppressive, insipid."

Religion is irrelevant when it ignores science and when it does not stand up against powers of injustice, whether they are corporate powers pillaging nature and destroying our climate, media powers peddling entertainment addictions and distractions, or religious bigotry masquerading as "tradition" in opposition to homosexuals or women and their rights.

When religion puts people to sleep in church because reading prayers from a book and fumbling through page after page to find them is, well, dull, it precipitates its own demise. The opposite of dull is interesting and alive and lively. Why not engage in worship that truly draws in the new art forms of our day, that includes rather than excludes the body—that encourages dancing our prayers instead of reading them?

Religion does not have to be dull. It chooses to be. Why? I think of the holy and great Bishop Casigalida whose diocese was the Amazon and how he created a special Mass with black Brazilians using their music and their culture and dance, but know-it-alls in the Curia forbade him to do so again after just one celebration.

How is religion oppressive? It is oppressive of women when it forbids them to hold leadership roles even though the early church championed them and counted them among the earliest followers of Jesus. One of his most startlingly breakthrough teachings was the gesture of welcoming women and entrusting them, as he did to Mary Magdalene, with authentic leadership roles. (13.217-222) The first Christian theologian, Paul, announced that "in Christ" there is no distinction of "male and female." What happened to this foundational teaching? Male clericalism replaced the revolutionary teachings of Jesus so that today only so-called "secular" society is advancing women's roles and justice toward women while the Church hierarchy lives in denial.

Religion was oppressive toward science when it locked up Galileo in 1633, forcing him to sign a confession denouncing his scientific discoveries. In the same way it is oppressive today when it denounces gay love while, once again, ignoring what science has to say on the subject.

Religion is oppressive when it silences 105 theologians and infects other thinkers with fear that obstructs thinking and promotes falling in line and obeying.

Religion is oppressive when it tolerates priestly pedophilia, spends hundreds of millions of dollars on lawyers to interfere with civil trials against pedophile priests instead of providing victims with support they so need.

You get the picture. The power of religion cannot be denied (liberals underestimate its power). It can be used to liberate or to oppress. Unfortunately, it is not always working on behalf of liberation.

"Insipid." Heshel, a poetic wordsmith, picked an interesting word to indict oppressive religion. Webster's Dictionary defines insipid as "tasteless" and "lacking in qualities that interest, stimulate or challenge; dull, flat, vapid, jejune, banal, inane and "devoid of qualities that make for spirit and character." Insipid is the opposite of "zestful." Yes, Heschel reminds us that religion can bring about its own insipidness. Many in the hierarchy and priesthood today do not even know their own tradition, or have the slightest understanding of mysticism or the Cosmic Christ or Creation Spirituality or the great souls like Hildegard of Bingen, Meister Eckhart, Julian of Norwich, Thomas Merton, Howard Thurman and more.

"When faith is completely replaced by creed..." Faith is not just creed; it is not a list of doctrines. Faith in the Bible is about trust. It is not about head tripping around centuries-old formulations of dogmas; it is about living with trust and living deeply, pursuing lives of purpose and commitment, of peace and of justice, of creativity and gratitude, compassion and generosity. How much easier it is to run a church on creed instead of on trust of spirit and trust that the Spirit is still alive and well, still at work in birthing new versions of community and new expressions of compassion in the world. Creed has been held up during the new inquisition (as it was in the old) to destroy all signs of new birth and fresh ideas and new life in the church. Creed has been used as a bludgeon to abort thinking and therefore theology in the church. Faith is something else and it endures where trust endures. It is ironic that a church that proclaims its opposition to abortion so loudly in fact is busy aborting life and signs of live, creativity and imagination everywhere it turns.

"Worship by discipline..." We have already discussed the dullness of worship but Heschel nails it when he notes how discipline enforcers can readily kill worship and stifle the spirit in worship. This has occurred countless times in the dark sanctums of the Curial netherlands where bureaucrats shoot down any possible imagination applied to Liturgy and where they even take glee in undoing translations in the vernacular to replace them with more Latin-sounding phrases. The first reform at Vatican II was the reform of the Liturgy and the document embodying it was heralded as a "magna carta of the laity." Today that magna carta is buried, gone the way of the original Magna Carta (which the pope at the time condemned). There is no room whatsoever for creativity in liturgy today.

"Love by habit..." Love is always in the now. Love is always particular as well as generic. Because we loved yesterday does not suffice for loving today. Love is not by rote, it demands something new and fresh of us daily. And sometimes it demands taking stands and being strong in the face of diversity. Love includes justice, in the Jewish tradition there is no love without justice. Eckhart put this wonderfully when he said there is only love between equals, never between masters and slaves, so we must be making justice happen or we are not engaged in love. And love is an engagement, a commitment, a decision to act. It is not done by rote but by applying ourselves daily to finding the good and the beautiful that indeed bring love alive in us. I think you put this memorably when you say "to love is much more than feeling tenderness or a certain emotion once in a while. It's a total challenge to creativity! No one knows how to love; we learn every day." (10.53f)

"When the crisis of today is ignored because of the splendor of the past..." It is heartening to hear you speak out about today's needs and not yesteryear's splendors and to see you preferring simple living even as pope to stylish "Paris Match" papal pomp and circumstance. Surely that is more in keeping with Francis' and Jesus' spirit than are the silly and outdated splendors of a Vatican of past days. Can you keep up this symbolism? I wish you luck. More important, can you keep today's crises always before you and as primary? Because that will be your biggest ally in resisting the splendors of the past, that and surrounding yourself with allies who share these values and are not in the Vatican to build their egos and massage their narcissistic souls. Today's crises include of course the earth and climate crisis, the unemployment crisis, the crisis of cynicism and despair, the crisis of unjust economic and gender divisions, the crisis of war and expenditures for war, the crisis of youth ignored and without elders, the crisis of loneliness, poverty and neglect. I know you know these crises and I am confident they and not splendors of the past will be what matters in your vocation.

"When faith becomes an heirloom rather than a living fountain..." Faith as heirloom, not merely an inheritance we are supposed to lock up and keep unsullied (and unused), to pass on untouched and untouched up and undeveloped to others. At the Vatican most people experience church as a museum. Faith as a "deposit" (favorite Canon Law language) as if it were something we visit in a bank vault once in a while, something all locked up never to be stirred, invested, put to work, reinvented or adapted to the language and culture of a new generation. Much preferable is the language of Saint John Henry Newman, a contemporary of Charles Darwin of the "development of doctrine," or we might say the evolution of doctrine. Doctrine has its place for humans who have to put experiences (the starting point of all faith) into words and then into categories for sharing with others, thus doctrines. But a doctrine is only a means and a doctrine is never to be frozen on ice or locked in a vault as if its value increases with age and pristineness.

Doctrines expand and evolve just like all beings and ideas do when we grow as individuals and communities over the course of time. As we ponder issues and challenges over the years and apply them in practice, we learn more about them, we see them from a variety of angles and under different illumination, watching new depths emerge as we too mature. What Rilke said about growing older—"I can see more deeply into paintings now"—we might apply to doctrines as well. They grow on us and we grow with them— provided we are not stuck in literalism or "lock them in a vault of deposit for safekeeping" mentality. So all doctrines evolve as we evolve and as the church, i.e. the people living them evolve. Can we see more deeply into doctrines now?

Thus faith is truly, in Heshel's words, a "living fountain," something wet and green and juicy (to use Hildegard's language) that refreshes, sustains, gives life, as does a fountain of fresh, flowing cold water. Thomas Aquinas says that the difference between living waters and stagnant waters is that the former connects to the Source. A living fountain does not contain stagnant water but moving waters, alive waters, fresh waters, not banked and deposited waters. It is from these that we drink heartily when we drink authentic faith. These waters assist our trusting.

"When religion speaks only in the name of authority rather than with the voice of compassion..." For thirty-five years the Roman Catholic Church has been speaking almost solely with the voice of authority: "Believe this because I tell you to; Believe this or you are not a Catholic; Do not even speak about women priests or you will be silenced and excommunicated." Consider how Fr. Roy Bourgeois was recently dismissed from the Maryknoll order after forty years of brave witness including jail terms for standing up to the School of the Americas which was a training ground for sadistic soldiers sent by Latin American dictators to learn the arts of torture; or two bishops of Australia dismissed after daring to raise the subject.

Obey, obey, obey. That is the only "theology" I see in

studying the sects that have been pushed so hard by the Vatican of late: Opus Dei, Communion and Liberation, and the Legion of Christ (which boasted a special vow of never speaking badly about the founder who turned out to be a pervert beyond measure). Obey, obey, obey—that is the very definition of fascism. Its patriarchal message of control and domination is all that matters, its image of God as a punitive father is perverse and it in turn gives legitimacy to punitive attitudes of "superiors"—all that plus sexism is found wherever fascism reigns. An ideology of obedience and authority is no substitute for theology. And it is miles from anything Jesus taught or lived.

Such ideology is the polar opposite of compassion, which is what Jesus taught. As theologian Dorothy Soelle puts it, the opposite of obedience is…solidarity. Yes, we are here to live lives of solidarity, especially with the poor and oppressed. Community and gatherings of solidarity are key to undoing authority-based religion. Compassion is the expression of true solidarity for it is not feeling alone but action we take to share the mutual joy and suffering that is our lot as humans. It is our struggle to relieve one another's suffering from injustice that causes so much pain; but it is also our shared desire to celebrate life and its joys. That, too, is compassion. As Meister Eckhart taught, "what happens to another, whether it be a joy or a sorrow, happens to me."

We are in this together at the deep levels of shared joy and shared sorrow. There lies our solidarity. But Eckhart, working out of the Jewish and Biblical tradition also taught that "compassion means justice" and "compassion is where peace and justice kiss." Compassion has a hard side to it. It is not just about mercy as you seemed to imply in a recent talk citing Walter Kasper. It is also about justice.

Some enemies of liberation theology cozied up to the

CIA (who, as you may recall, were busy overthrowing the duly elected president of Chile, Salvador Allende, and installing the murderous dictator Augusto Pinochet, and overthrowing the government of Argentina to install an atrocious military junta that tortured and killed 30,000 innocent people) to label Liberation theology "Marxist." This is just language the CIA wanted wielded all over Latin America. But it was not so. The Bible, even as Eckhart knew it in the fourteenth century, insists on love and justice being one. Marx may well have derived that from the Bible in fact. But that does not make Liberation theology Marxist. If anything it makes Marx Biblical!

Without compassion in all of its meanings Heschel warns us "religion's message becomes meaningless."

With all my heart I hope your papacy is one of compassion in its fullest and richest meanings and an example to other institutions of our world that compassion matters. And justice matters. You have said so yourself in the following words: "In the fact of grave forms of social and economic injustice, of political corruption, of ethnic cleansing, of demographic extermination, and destruction of the environment...surges the need for a radical personal and social renewal that is capable of ensuring justice, solidarity, honesty, and transparency." (10.48f)

Can you help us move beyond meaningless religion? We hope you can and we are here to assist that process, for this is what the people of God have always been striving for.

3 FRANCIS, THE COSMIC CHRIST AND THE FUTURE OF OUR SPECIES

Dear Pope Francis:

It is clear to everyone who has ever heard of Francis of Assisi that his heart was centered on the "glory" (his word) of creation, on the revelation that creation bestows on us daily whether through animals or birds, or through Mother Earth and her bounty, or through Brother Sun and the heat and light and energy it bestows on us, or through sister water in the rivers and oceans and lakes that gift us so with both beauty and survival essentials. In his great praise poem that we know as the Canticle of the Sun he never mentions Jesus' name once. But he does talk about "glory" which as you know is a technical Biblical word for divine numinosity or splendor or "sheen" (Aquinas' word) that burns in every being. Glory (*doxa* in Greek) is a word for the Cosmic Christ and that is why Francis is so at ease in calling the sun "Lord" because "Lord" too is a title for the Cosmic Christ. Francis, your chosen namesake, was a champion of the Cosmic Christ.

So too was another Italian saint and mystic, Thomas Aquinas, about whom G. K. Chesterton wrote that he should be remembered as "Thomas of Creation." These two saints, Francis and Aquinas, only one generation apart, were different personalities entirely; Francis a taster and explorer of the holiness of creation who lived a simple but often ascetic life style; and Aquinas, a more educated and intellectually dazzling person who, while steeped in learning, never wandered from his basic premise that "revelation comes in two volumes, nature and the Bible." He gave nature its due—it is not a mere object "out there" to serve human needs—it is also a source of grace and revelation (and, as Meister Eckhart would say one generation after Aquinas, "nature is grace"). Aquinas pursued the study of scientists like Aristotle because he was so serious about the role nature plays in ethics and spirituality.

Different as Francis and Aquinas were, they shared the regard for appreciating, honoring and reverencing the God of creation who made creation "good" and indeed "very good" (Genesis 1). They both were born and raised in Italy, a land blessed with rich earth, sun, hills and soil. They were giants in their day and remain so in ours, for framing a proper praise and love of Mother Earth and all creatures. Both deserve to be remembered as Green Prophets for our perilous times when Earth is undergoing catastrophes unmatched in sixty-five million years, most brought upon us by narcissism and human anthropocentrism, institutional, corporate, and media greed, lack of education, and alas, by religion itself.

For centuries, the preoccupation within Western Christianity with Augustine's neurotic question, "am I saved?," has set religion on a path of self-destruction and self-absorption that neither Francis nor Aquinas would recognize. It has brought us to this perilous moment when our species' and millions of other species' sustainability is in question. Religion must change. Education must change. Business must change. Economics must change. Politics must change. I appreciate your passionate language when you say justice must be "extremely creative."

What an opportunity faces you in your new position as pope and in Francis' name to alert humanity and its cultural institutions—beginning with the Church—to our own folly as well as our potential to change and change deeply: to create and to co-create a new direction that throws off militarism and reptilian brain domination in favor of our mammal brains with their special capacity for compassion, kinship and family. It is significant surely that in both Hebrew and Arabic the word for "compassion" derives from the word for "womb." We people are the womb-species: we are the ones who have a biological destiny to bring justice and compassion to the planet. How are we doing? Isn't this what unites the teachings of Jesus and Buddha and Isaiah and Muhammad and Black Elk too? So many messengers from the Creator urging us to bring compassion alive! How slow we have been to imbibe these messages. Time is running out. Hopefully you, in Francis' name, can facilitate a turnaround.

The Church must do what Francis and you talk about: simplify, simplify, simplify. Strip down to the essentials and let go of the centuries of accretions that have rendered it more like a museum than a living entity. A museum with unhappy watchdog guardians of an idol called "orthodoxy." How sure I am that were Jesus alive today he would reenact his sweeping of the money lenders from the temple by sweeping these pseudo-religious hypocrites from the spiritually hollow halls of the Vatican castle.

What the young the world over are calling for is an end to religion as usual, and a commitment to putting life first.

Now is the time to worship a God of Life, and reject the Gods of religion or ideology. It is time for more authentic spirituality and less contrived religion. We need more practices to calm our frenzied reptilian brains, and a church that supports those practices instead of amassing wealth, arcane rules, power, and dated dogmas. In embracing instead these calming practices, let us put the earth ahead of stale religious comforts. It is so important and so significant at this time that we hear elders and the young agreeing on such basic values.

Another witness in our Christian tradition to the radical sacredness of creation is our Sister Hildegard, recently canonized as a Saint and named a Doctor of the Church. meaning surely that we ought to be listening to her at this pivotal time in human and planetary history. How thoroughly imbued she was with the Cosmic Christ and a Creation Spirituality perspective even before Francis (who was born two years after Sister Hildegard died). For her the "Word" (Logos or Sophia or the Cosmic Christ) is present in all creation as the power of fecundity and creativity. It is "living, being, spirit, all verdant greening, all creativity." It "manifests itself in every creature" yet it is "indivisible from God." (11.12) The Cosmic Christ is the light in all things (and today's physics confirms there are photons or light waves in every atom in the universe) and according to Hildegard "God's word is in all creation visible and invisible." The Cosmic Christ awareness attests to the holiness in every rock, river, tree, whale, fish, horse, bird, cloud, and human. It helps us retrieve a sense of the sacred that is all around us or in Jesus' words, the "kingdom of God" that is within us and among us. Surely we ought to be listening to her now.

This same tradition of the Cosmic Christ is found richly developed in the work of my Dominican brother Meister Eckhart who followed in the footsteps of Thomas

Aquinas when he declared that "every creature is a word of God and a book about God." Thus, like Francis and Aquinas, he is equating the sacred book of nature with the Bible itself—both are sources of revelation. Modern consciousness, so imbued with anthropocentrism, has lost this sense of the omnipresence of Divinity in all things; it has substituted a sterile and distant theism (God in the sky) for a live and present and immanent panentheism (God in all things and all things in God). But all our great creation mystics were panentheists, as Mechtild of Magdeburg said: "The day of my spiritual awakening was the day I saw God in all things and all things in God."

This rich and often neglected tradition of the Cosmic Christ being present in all things also puts new life and meaning into what for many is the dark and remote icon of the crucifixion. The Christ is not only in Jesus—it is in all things. Therefore when a rain forest gets cut down or a species goes extinct, the Christ is being crucified all over again. We need to cease the often sentimental and narcissistic pieties built on the "I have crucified my Savior 2000 years ago" mentality and get real. We are crucifying the Christ when we participate in the destruction of the earth and its creatures through our neglect, greed, or lack of caring. The same is true when humans are made sick or die as a result of injustice or indifference; each time these prevail, the Christ is crucified all over again.

Another gift to our times from this spiritual tradition is its celebration of our powers of creativity. I believe creativity is the one attribute our species has going for it. With the challenges of our times, creativity needs to rise to the occasion like never before. Humans are intensely creative—that is why we have taken over the planet in 100,000 years—which is something no other species ever even came close to doing that. It took dinosaurs millions of years to dominate the planet, plants too. Why are humans so in charge? Because of our immense intellect, imagination, and creativity. Having taken over the planet, we are now killing it. Our creativity is not matched by our wisdom apparently. As Einstein wrote after the secrets of splitting the atom were uncovered by the most creative minds on the planet, "everything has changed, save our modes of thinking, thus we drift to unparalleled catastrophe." Humans do evil. Creativity needs channeling, it needs contours, it needs direction. That is exactly what justice and compassion provide—directions and guidelines for our creativity. Francis, wouldn't your namesake and shouldn't the Church hold any human endeavor to this fundamental moral test: "Is our creativity leading to justice or injustice, to balance or imbalance, to sustainability or unsustainability, to the healthy future of Mother Earth or to its vastly reduced potential for our descendants?"

Our divine-like creativity needs to seek out the beauty we can make, the communities we can build, the healing we can effect, the joy we can generate, the celebrations we can birth, the remembering we can invoke, the rituals we can share, the work by which we can employ others, the gardens we can grow, the food we can harvest, the forgiveness we can bring about. Meister Eckhart teaches that what we give birth to is always another Christ. At a Christmas Mass he preached this message: "What good is it to me if Mary gave birth to the Son of God 1400 years ago and I don't give birth to the Son of God in my person, my time, my culture? We are all meant to be mothers of God." Yes, we are not only other Christs, but other Marys. How are we doing?

Another champion of the Cosmic Christ besides the medieval geniuses we cite is your more recent twentieth-century brother Jesuit, the scientist, poet and mystic, Father Teilhard de Chardin Teilhard taught at my alma mater, the Institut Catholique de Paris, and was one of the first theologians to use the exact phrase, "Cosmic Christ." His daring marriage of modern physics to a Cosmic Christ spirituality was expressed so: "The cosmos is fundamentally and primarily living...Christ, through his Incarnation, is internal to the world...rooted in the world, even in the heart of the tiniest atom....Nothing seems to me more vital, from the point of view of human energy, than the appearance and eventually, the systematic cultivation of such a 'cosmic sense.'" (7.23,130f) Teilhard's vision was of an end to dualisms, such as those preached by the recent popes, that pit a so-called "secular world" against a Christian world. Such dualisms give way to feelings of impotence and despair, and to fundamentalist temptations to imagine "we are saved and they are not, we are the righteous and they are sinners." Teilhard also spoke directly to this issue when he declared that "by virtue of the creation and, still more, the Incarnation, nothing here below is profane for those who know how to see." (5.66)

Teilhard incorporated this theology of the Cosmic Christ into his understanding of worship when he wrote: "Over every living thing which is to spring up, to grow, to flower to ripen during this day say again the words: 'This is my body.'" And he applied the Cosmic Christ theology to the crucifixion with these words: "And over every death-force which awaits in readiness to corrode, to wither, to cut down, speak again your commanding words which express the supreme mystery of faith: 'This is my Blood.'" (8.23) Do you see how a Cosmic Christ theology puts meaning back into the rich archetypes and rituals of our ancestors?

Yet Teilhard felt the Cosmic Christ theology was little appreciated in his time when he observed that "this third nature of Christ (neither human nor divine, but Cosmic)— has not noticeably attracted the explicit attention of the faithful or of theologians." Indeed, it didn't take long for the Vatican to try to banish him to China for his "new" ideas. But today, thanks to new Biblical scholarship, we are finally rediscovering how rooted the Cosmic Christ theology was in the very origins of the Christian movement. The renowned New Testament scholar, Bruce Chilton, writes that for St. Paul Christ is not only cosmic but "metacosmic." Paul incorporates the earliest hymns of the church into his letters and they are hymns of how Christ "connects all things in heaven and on earth"— hymns to the Cosmic Christ therefore. Thus a theology of the Cosmic Christ is not new—it is, rather, something lost.

Lost yet found again by Hildegard and Francis, Aquinas, Eckhart and Teilhard and today's eloquent writers and teachers such as Father Thomas Berry and cosmologist Brian Swimme. Together they have brought forth a revived understanding of the holiness of the universe by translating the new creation story that science has provided about the 13.8 billion year journey of the universe. The new cosmology they present once again sets our human story in a sacred context, indeed a sacramental context that has great implications for a renewed sense of sacrament.

Your Jesuit brother Teilhard offered a critique of contemporary religion when he wrote: "Because it is not exalted by a sufficiently passionate admiration of the universe, our religion is becoming enfeebled." The Cosmic Christ archetype renders sacred all our relationships. Life itself, with all its valleys and mountains, ecstasies and emptying, becomes sacred. The journey itself becomes a sacred journey.

What is the church? It is the people on this sacred journey. It is not buildings or bureaucracies or religious potentates or hierarchy as such but people on the sacred journey of life. This is why Hildegard of Bingen says that "the Word," i.e. the Cosmic Christ, is head of the church and the Lord or Cosmic Christ is found in everyone and every being. Such an image of church is non-hierarchical and non ladder-like. It is circular and close to the earth. It is eye to eye. Indeed, it is the difference between riding in a special limousine and simply taking a bus or subway to your destination—a personal habit of simplicity that you reflect so well. As you know, Jesus said: "Do not look here or there for the Kingdom of God, but within and among you." The church is a verb and not a noun; a journey and not a destination; a process and not a thing or institution. We have to be on guard against ecclesial idol worship on a daily basis.

I am impressed as I write this that you are being so slow to move into the palaces of the Vatican. You seem sensitive to what I am writing about. Yes, perhaps more may be at stake in your obvious reluctance to take up residence in one of the last palaces on earth and to do so in Jesus' name. Good for you! Francis and Jesus would both resist as you are resisting. Surely there is a simpler place to bear a more authentic witness to Jesus' name and work than the Vatican palaces in their current state.

The medicine for a religion of control, projection, fear and enfeeblement is to return to experience. That is why mysticism is at the heart of the renewal of religion and always has been—as Carl Jung noted, "only the mystic brings what is creative to religion itself."

As humans finally wake up to the destruction we have wrought against the earth our religions will become more humble and will link arms more readily. There is health in diversity and we all share a universal call to work for the common good and for future generations. We will move from religion to spirituality, from noun to verb, from ecclesiolatry to experience of healing through both contemplative and active practices.

People today are seeking maps and paths for the journey that are tested and true, archetypal and deep, useful and simple to employ. I invite you to consider the Four Paths of Creation Spirituality in the work that lies ahead of you. I noticed that early in your dialog with Rabbi Skorka you talked about how important the concept of path was to your understanding of spirituality and you returned to this theme time and again. In this I see all the more reason to share with you the Four Paths that I believe articulate the depth of our shared journeys. These paths should lie at the heart of any "new evangelization."

The first path is the Via Positiva, our falling in love with life and the goodness of things, the experience of awe ("radical amazement" in Rabbi Heshel's language), wonder, delight, and joy. It is a path of praise, even if, in poet Leonard Cohen's words, our Halleluia is at times "cold and broken"—it is still a song of praise.

The second Path is the Via Negativa, a way of silence and nothingness and emptiness but also of suffering and grief and letting go and letting be. "We sink eternally from letting go to letting go into the One," observes Meister Eckhart.

The Third Path is the Via Creativa, the path of creativity and of birthing. It is born of the love we learn in Path One and the emptying we undergo in Path Two. In it we become like Mary, the receptors for the Spirit of creativity, or, as Aquinas put it: "the same Spirit that hovered over the waters at the beginning of creation hovers over the mind of the artist at work."

The Fourth Path is the Via Transformativa, the way of Justice-making and Compassion. It is a sort of culmination of the other paths for no prophet ever existed who was not an artist of social change (Gandhi leading marches to the sea or Martin Luther King filling the jails). Every prophet works out of love (first path) and is emptied time and again (second path) but is called upon to be imaginative and to enlist the moral imagination of others (third path). You capture the depth of the Via Transformativa when you say: "An act of justice that becomes concrete in helping one's neighbor is a prayer." (10.61)

All four paths are paths of prayer.

Creation Spirituality can be transformative for these times because it treats the people of God as adults and not simply passive consumers of pieties from on high. By bringing alive the mystic and the prophet in us all, it honors the contemplative and the activist in each of us. The journey along these Four Paths forms a spiral that culminates in our engaging in the work of the kingdom, of justice and compassion, so that more may share the gifts of Life. The spiral is thus open ended and ever expansive; it begins anew with new people at the banquet table of life ready to imbibe all that the Via Positiva and life have to offer.

4 FRANCIS, YOUTH, AND THE QUEST FOR INTERGENERATIONAL WISDOM

Dear Pope Francis:

Francis of Assisi was a young man of twenty-four years when the deep inspiration to "repair my church," struck him, an inspiration that led to a break with his father. He banded with brothers and sisters like the communes of the day he had observed on travels with his father through Italy and southern France. Clare was only eighteen years old when she abandoned her privileged family to join Francis' band after being moved by Francis' preaching. Her sister Catherine was only sixteen when she joined Clare in disavowing her clan to follow Francis.

Francis was in touch with all that was young and new in the manner that Meister Eckhart encouraged: "God is novissimus (the newest thing in the universe)." In stark contrast, today's church seems very tired, un-new, indeed un-young, if not actually anti-young. Can you change that? Here are some ideas.

It is more and more clear that young people are leaving the church and organized religion in droves. This is not just a European or North American issue—it is happening in Latin America also. This is in part because a new generation has come of age in a post-modern world where so many of our institutional structures (including but not limited to religion) have developed in a modern context. That creates a huge disconnect between older ones who see the world through modern eyes and consciousness and younger ones whose post-modern perspective yields a different reality. (12. 109-126)

I have been working with Adam Bucko, a thirty-five year old prophet who works with street youth and young adults in New York City. He has created a marvelous program for youth living on the streets. His organization is called "The Reciprocity Foundation" and a documentary about his work was nominated for an Emmy last year. Adam's approach is to bring creativity and spiritual practice alive in young people's lives, many of whom have been abused in various ways even before they started to live on the streets. In our book called *Occupy Spirituality: A Radical Vision for a New Generation* we engage in a conversation about young people and their attitudes toward religion and spirituality, comparing what we have observed from our vantage points, as both of us have worked with young people in our various ministries over the years. We also incorporate results of surveys and interviews we conducted with young people around the United States.

One thing we have learned is that they are very aware of the ecological crisis, corruption in the institutional church, irrelevance of much of the Church's teaching and messaging, and their own deep need and yearning for spirituality, but left wanting by the Church's failure to deliver. Today's generation knows when it is being talked down to, when, though adults, they are treated as children.

When it comes to sex for example, they simply don't carry the awful burden of homophobia that so weighs down many older people and most prelates. Young adults I know have made the wise and mature decision that they are in charge of their bodies and they do not need celibate or so called celibate clergy telling them what their sexual expression can or cannot be about, especially when the teaching behind that ethic derives not from Jesus or his Jewish tradition but from a fourth century priest named Augustine who lived a profligate life as a young man and then taught sex is a sin (because one "loses control"). Augustine's position that sex must be justified by baby-making on every occasion does not resonate with today's young adults.

The pedophile scandals among the clergy have been a topic of discussion for two decades. Young adults question whether church is even a safe place, let alone a source of justice and compassion. The response of the hierarchy has done little to assuage this concern and I know parents with who won't endanger their children by putting them in harm's way of a church where prelates like Cardinal Mahony of Los Angeles make fervent efforts to cover up priestly abuse with disregard towards victims. Only in the past few months have the facts begun to be made public about the mountains of documents he hid from investigators for over twelve years and the amount of money he spent for lawyers and others to continue covering up the cover up. Earlier this year HBO aired a widely acclaimed documentary focusing on one case in Milwaukee, Wisconsin where a priest abused over 200 deaf students over twenty-three years when he was finally removed in 1974 from the deaf school. The documentary, which received a lot of attention in the United States, shows that Cardinal Ratzinger, then head of the CDF, a congregation responsible for wayward priests, knew about these cases but did not act. In fact, the serial abuser from Milwaukee was allowed to stay in the priesthood and be buried as a priest in good standing.

Those are just a few of the realities of pedophile priests and their cover up by the hierarchy surely has something to do with the distance young adults are putting between themselves and organized religion.

Youth do not need a lot of lecturing from elders. They need opening circles of sharing and mutual respect. They can't hear long lists of "Don'ts" uttered by distant heirarchs, and they won't read catechisms created by lazy prelates who insult their intelligence, treating them like children. Can you lead a new way? It was touching to see you wash the feet of young offenders in a juvenile jail on Holy Thursday. It seems you are sensitive to the needs of the young, an issue that was surely dear to Francis. You demonstrated a similar sensitivity in your recent beatification ceremony of Rev. Giuseppe "Pino" Puglisi of Palermo whom you praised as a martyr and "exemplary priest" for standing up to the Mafia and helping young people resist recruitment by organized crime. Bravely do you speak and concretely to the exploitation of young the world over, when you say, "behind this exploitation and slavery are the mafias."[7]

The young carry their own wisdom, especially this generation that is facing so much hardship, so much degradation of the earth, so few offers of full employment and yet have embraced powerful new ways of communicating, learning and celebrating. Allow me to

---

[7] Frances D'Emilio, "Pope urges Mafiosi to stop exploitation of others," *Yahoo! News*, May 26, 2013.

share with you just one testimony from a young adult arrested while meditating at an Occupy demonstration in my city of Oakland, California. Pancho Ramos-Stierle writes the following: Modern poverty "boasts two kinds of slaves: the intoxicated—the prisoner to the addiction of consumption, and those who aspire to get intoxicated—the prisoner of envy." What does the Occupy movement mean to him? "We are the early adopters of a revolution in values, and we are the evidence that the totalitarianism of corporate capitalism, the machine that has devastated the planet and human beings—we are the demonstration that system doesn't work and that we need a new system...It is time for the spiritual to get active and the activist people to get spiritual so that we can have total revolution of the human spirit...We need to combine this inner revolution with the outer revolution to have the total revolution of the spirit." (4.xxvii) You see what allies we and Francis and others have among many young people today?

Young people seeing visions are enthralled by adventure. They yearn for adventure. Scientific philosopher Alfred North Whitehead warned that "the death of religion comes with the repression of the high hope of adventure." What is adventurous in today's ecclesial preoccupations and agenda I ask? When one claims to have all the answers to the only important questions, as do catechisms which are little more than regurgitations of canon laws, no adventure is suggested or elicited. More importantly, what might be adventurous is ignored altogether.

Here I offer some possibilities where you could help lead. Nature and grace, science and spirituality, is an adventure, a frontier unfolding in our time. So too is deep ecumenism. So too is awareness of our sexuality and its diversity. So too is the call to new forms of economics, religion, worship, education and service. Work that provides an ethical challenge such as Engineers Without Borders is another example of spiritual adventure in our time.

All these areas need reinventing today and demand daring and risk and choice-making. As an elder I invite you to support the younger generation to see new forms and models take root. Surely the papacy, with its immediate ties to the global media for example, could be a voice for the voiceless and a voice for the younger visionaries who see it as their vocation to reinvent forms of finance, education, and religion. You are currently putting forth a fine model in your recent pronouncements on employment and the welfare of workers, words that are actually being listened to and heard by these young people who desire nothing more than an economic structure that works for everyone.

As more and more young adults choose to live in community (often because of economic limitations since full-time work is so hard to find), much spiritual renewal is taking place and will take place. Within the context of intimacy in community many lessons of conviviality, sharing, growing one's food, cooking together, respect for difference, political organizing, meditation are learned. And they offer a slower pace to living. The Italian "decrescita felice" (happy de-growth) movement today surely smacks of similar values.

Today's youth are not waiting for marching orders from priests, bishops, or popes. They are putting their consciences to work with great imagination. What might happen if you, in the spirit of your namesake Francis, would acknowledge their work, listen deeply and support their adventure by engaging it? In short, I would love to see the Church hierarchy start acting like responsible elders and learn to listen again and support the Spirit speaking and acting through the young.

One adventure worth undertaking today is that which drew me to a ministry I have been involved in for the past sixteen years. It is an experiment supported by the Anglican church to render liturgy and worship fun and inviting once again. I am talking about bringing the body back to worship and about honoring the young by inviting them to incorporate their new art forms such as DJ-ing and VJ-ing and Rap and break-dancing and rave into the liturgy. The results have been deeply encouraging—it is not only young people but people of all ages who are hungry for worship that elicits beauty and participation. The modern age began with the printing press and so it has reduced worship pretty much to texts; but post-modern consciousness today prefers context and images to text.

We call this adaptation of the rave celebrations "The Cosmic Mass" and we are proud of what we are doing and eager to share it with the larger church. The main reason I became an Anglican priest, after Cardinal Ratzinger expelled me from the Dominican Order where I was a member in good standing for thirty-four years, was to work with young people to reinvent forms of worship. Our Cosmic Mass does that and I want you to know that it has much to offer those eager for worship experiences that transform.

Clearly what we are doing is of universal (i.e. catholic) interest since the young people world over are finding new (and ancient, pre-modern) languages in which to celebrate. Surely dance is one of those languages and so too is electronic music or what we call the "urban shamanism" of the electronic drum which so engages the first chakra as all drum and dancing does. How important it is that we move from prayer taking place in the head to prayer that take place throughout the body! How will we ever be instruments to heal the earth if we are not in touch with the earth? By dancing on the earth we re-learn reverence for it and honor it. All this can and ought to happen in worship as we have demonstrated over the past sixteen years.

Our Cosmic Masses are very ecumenical—we have had participants who are Jews and Buddhists and Hindus and Native American and Muslim as well as Christians of many stripes. Isn't this as it should be? Shouldn't humans be worshiping together? We have sponsored over ninety Cosmic Masses in 16 years. This summer we will celebrate a Cosmic Mass at a Sounds True gathering of 1000 people in the mountains of Colorado. No doubt participants will include Protestants and Catholics but also Jews and Buddhists, Hindus and more. In other words, it is a catholic gathering, a universal gathering. Such is the promise of working with young people and the new languages they bring to worship. We once did a mass for 1400 persons at the University of Colorado and our DJ, who was only 28 years old, had conducted rave celebrations in Johannesburg, Paris, London, Berlin, New York, Bangkok, Tokyo, Los Angeles. In other words, rave is already catholic. It is universal. Why should the Church not be interested in how it can revitalize worship for people of all ages and cultures?

It is my experience that youth bring hope and humor, laughter and often joy, into the room. Lama Surya Das, who has worked extensively with young people in New York, talks well of the reciprocity between young and elders, how one gifts the other, when he says: "When I read or listen to the world news, it can be depressing and cause me to wonder where it's all leading...But whenever I talk with a young person, I am irrationally filled with hope, optimism, certainty and delight." He is so right. The young light up the room for us all. They do bring hope and laughter even in the midst of what they know is a very serious moment in human and planetary history.

Francis was all for starting Christianity over—that is why his followers and others consciously rejected the term "Christendom" (or "Christianitas" in Latin) in favor of a return to "evangelical poverty." They chose to reject the imperial church of Constantine and the privileges of the monastic/feudal establishment that owned so much property and controlled so much of the wealth and decision making of his era. As historian Pere Chenu puts it, "Neither St. Francis nor St. Dominic belonged to this 'Christendom.'" Many people today, young and not so young, are throwing off the word "Christian." Recently, at a retreat in Bingen, Germany, where I was presenting about our sister Hildegard of Bingen, a participant in her fifties, said simply, "I am embarrassed by the word 'Christian.'"

Thus we look for new language—just as Francis looked for it in the early thirteenth century. "Christ Path" is a term I am currently using because, unlike "Christianity," it is Biblical and traceable to our earliest sources and it does not necessarily carry the baggage of some 1900 years of often dubious practice in Jesus' name.[8]

To your Francis and his movement as well as to my Dominic and his, there was a strong appeal to St. Peter speaking to the community of Jerusalem on the occasion of the First Pentecost (Acts 2:14-21), invoking the text of the prophet Joel. "On the day of the Lord, I will pour out my spirit upon all of humankind, and your sons and daughters will be prophets. Your young ones shall see

---

[8] I have recently teamed up with sacred activist and writer Andrew Harvey to conduct a series we call "Christ Path Seminar" to bring the teachings and values of Jesus alive again. See www.christpathseminar.org.

visions, and your old ones shall dream dreams." These words held a "special vigor for these generations" in the evangelical awakening of the late twelfth and early thirteen century, as the great scholar Pere Chenu points out.

They also hold for our times. All of humankind is capable of receiving spirit, regardless of their religious tradition; all are called to be prophets whose primary work Rabbi Heschel defines as "interference." Young people are seeing visions and hopefully some elders are still dreaming dreams. It is so important to listen to the dreams of young people and the questions they are asking especially in a moment in history as fraught as ours. Will we be able to survive as a species? Will we preserve the Earth and allow it to flourish? These are not trivial questions. Their answers require the in-put and hard work of the young as well some wisdom from the elders.

A grave danger of sentimentalizing looms at the invocation of St. Francis. One way to combat this temptation of imprisoning Francis in a birdbath is to set him in his historical context. The backdrop to his life offers deep insights pertinent to our own times, and I think it is important to take a moment to examine what your special namesake accomplished (and failed to accomplish) in his vocation.

I was blessed to study with the great historian of the twelfth and thirteenth century, the late and beautiful Pere Chenu (1895-1990), my Dominican brother who, as you may well be aware, was one of the significant theological sources and voices at the Second Vatican Council. He writes in his revered classic, *Nature, Man and Society in the Twelfth Century*, in great depth about the "revolution" that birthed Francis.

Chenu writes that Francis and his fellow revolutionaries

rejected the myth of Constantine, who had established "the papacy as heir of the Roman Empire...consecrated by a religious mission." (9.267) What became a spiritual insight in Francis' day remains a verdict of current Biblical scholarship. There is a new recognition that the Church took a decisive detour away from Gospel values when it inherited the empire in the fourth century and began to bless the very mechanisms common to all empires that drive them whether they are Roman, Spanish, Portuguese, German, English or American. In their colossal appetite for power and dominance, empires use religion more surely than they preach or live it.

As a citizen of Latin America you are well aware of the lacerations that the empire to the North has leveled on the back of the people of Central and South America, punishment from which you are still emerging. Who dares forget the conspiracy of Nixon and Kissinger to overthrow the duly elected government of Allende and replace it with the likes of Pinochet? Or that American gunships off of Brazil helped the military rulers of that country for years? Or that Nixon and Kissinger and Wall Street also helped to overthrow democracy in your own Argentina and to install the iron-fisted rule of the military junta that killed up to 30,000 citizens? When you've seen one empire you have seen them all.

Let us also remember, in invoking the spiritual genius of Francis of Assisi, that he and the movements from which he derived such as guilds, communes and fraternities of his day, rejected hierarchy and monasticism and their vertical models of obedience in favor of a more democratic way of governing. They "substituted a horizontal and fraternal agreement for vertical and paternalistic fidelity, and this agreement was affirmed not in a religious rite but in the solidarity of the 'brothers' and in democratic deliberation. And the new evangelists stupefied the feudal ecclesiastics with their bold claim that the new regime no less than the old was in accord with the faith, with the good news of the gospel, and with the love of charity." (9.265) Can you move from an ideology of obedience that has taken over the Vatican the past thirty-three years to a Franciscan understanding of fraternal and sororal solidarity? I hope so and pray you do.

Let us remember that Francis and his followers were allowed to preach even though they were not priests and especially to give witness to faith and morals ("verbum exhortationis"). Pope Innocent III made explicit the distinction between preaching doctrine and giving witness to faith and morals and "the pope gave Francis and his brothers permission to preach penance everywhere, provided that whoever was going to preach got approval from the blessed Francis. And to any of the brethren, layman or cleric, that had the spirit of God, he gave permission to preach." Not only did the layman Francis preach but Peter Waldo and Hildegard of Bingen, now saint and doctor of the Church, also preached.

Why turn our back on 51% of the human species, namely women, who can and ought to be invited to preach today? Shouldn't laity and young people including women be preaching today as well? This is part of the wisdom of small communities—that the Holy Spirit speaks through all who are trying to live the Gospel in difficult times and not just through those who have traveled a clerical journey.

We know how Francis absolutely resisted the traditional forms of religious life. He would not agree "to be diverted into the monastic or hermetic life" but rather, when Cardinal Ugolino arrived on the scene and urged him to return to the legislation of St. Benedict or St Augustine, Francis led the cardinal silently before his brothers and from the depths of his soul cried out: "My brothers, my brothers, God has called me by the way of simplicity and of humility, and He has pointed out this way as being the true way, both for me and for those who wish to believe me and imitate me. So don't talk to me about some rule or other, neither that of St. Benedict, nor of St. Augustine, nor of St. Bernard, nor about any life or way of living other than that which the Lord has mercifully shown and given to me." (9.258) Spoken as a true mystic, Francis trusted his inner experience more than that of heralded saints and ecclesial leaders.

What was that "true way" he was shown? It was the way of the primitive church. When Francis pleaded before Innocent III he said bluntly: "I do not come here with a new rule; my only rule is the gospel." As Chenu reminds us, "The particular opening of a new evangelical period was marked by an astute sensitivity to the appearance and to the forms of the primitive church. With its poverty and humility, the religious life of the primitive church became an ideal, indeed a sort of mystique, which engaged the productive energies of people." (9.239) The program, in line with Dominic's vision, was based on Luke 9:1-6 and 10:1-16. "Acting and preaching as had the master, going on foot, without gold and without silver, imitating in everything the way of the apostles." The prelates and monks of Francis' day were not so much lacking in zeal as they were "somehow unable to speak the same language as these Christian people." (9.245) The new wave spoke a common language with the people none of whom were in debt to the monastic/feudal establishment. So today, can you address all the people and not just the holders of keys to power in the financial, media, geopolitical and religious worlds? Can you imitate Francis in that regard? Can you speak to a post-modern generation?

Some other lessons we can learn from a serious historical critique of Francis and his times are the following:

1. The Gospel was the norm for proper Christian behavior in the reformation of Francis' day, not the established institutions (including religious ones). As Chenu says, "It was unmistakably the discovery of the gospel which lay behind this development of Christianity, and...there was a "rejection of 'rules' and traditional conformity in favor of a singular reliance upon the gospel." (9.231) Acts 4:32 was a classic text but Luke 10:1-12 even more so because it included preaching. It was this reaching out to others born into a new culture that was at the heart of this return to a vita apostolica. "Preaching, itinerant preaching—as opposed to monastic stability and as distinguished from episcopal preaching—was central to the new vita apostolica. After all, it was the apostolate which made the apostle: *vita vere apostolica* (the truly apostolic life)." (9.214)

2. It was lay people, not clerics, who advanced the Gospel values most rapidly. Francis was a lay person launching a lay movement (only later and contrary to his wishes did it become a clerical movement). "The new role of the laity was a logical and necessary outcome of the revolution in progress. Since the evangelical awakening took place not by a revision of existing institutions but by a return to the gospel that by-passed these institutions one could predict what its dynamics had to be: witness to the faith, fraternal love, poverty, the beatitudes—all these were to operate more spontaneously and sooner among laymen than among clerics, who were bound with an institutional framework." The crisis of the time was real. "Laymen everywhere took part in this upsurge"—practice was key with the lay people. "It represented a full-fledged vocation...The new role of the laity was a logical and necessary outcome of the revolution in progress." (9.219) Can we, can you in your role as Bishop of Rome and pope,

bypass many of our sclerotic institutions in favor of a return to the Gospels? Surely that is what the Second Vatican Council attempted to bring about.

3. Behind all the ferment, the "revolution" and the "renaissance" at work was a revolution in thinking about grace and nature and how to relate to an emerging new world view. Christians of the twelfth century "consciously faced up to the perennial problems of nature and grace, of the world and the gospel; and for them this problem was not so much an object of theological debate as it was the shifting, controverted, or bold expression of their encounter with a new society which they were having to penetrate as apostles...Throughout this century, the return to the primitive life of the church...inspired as well a new awareness of the ways that grace could take root in nature." (9.203)

A fresh view of nature and a new appreciation for science inspired much of the energy and visions that so moved a whole new generation. Says Chenu: "Another occurrence, more profound than these socio-economic ruptures—this time in men's minds—enlarged the context we are studying. During the twelfth century, there appeared an increasingly acute sensitivity to natural phenomena: to the harmony of the cosmos; to the place of man in this universe where his liberty asserted itself amidst certain determinisms of which he was aware; where he was himself a nature; where he tried to exercise his mastery in full consciousness of his own reason for being; where man's autonomy of action was experienced as the condition of his moral perfection, indeed of his religious value." (9.232)

Here the issue of context, so dear to post-modern awareness, is raised unequivocally. We are living in a time of a whole new cosmology—as were the believers of the twelfth century. It is truly pitiful how little the new cosmology has penetrated religion as it is practiced today and the Vatican of recent decades which seems to prefer anthropocentric naval gazing to gazing at the stars, the supernovas, the birth and resurrection of galaxies, all the wonders and graces with which the universe birthed us over 13.8 billion years ago. Here lies fertile ground for re-awakening the Via Positiva, that love of life and gratitude for life from which reverence is birthed.

Chenu comments that the new Christians saw the world as "an organic, homogenous ensemble, the observation of which was not only possible but worthwhile and satisfying. For the mind it was an exciting and precise exercise. Even before philosophy benefited from it, the imagination was astounded by it." The Gothic Cathedrals included images of nature's flora and fauna, green men, seasons and everyday events such as real people at work: "the carpenter; the wheelwright; the cloth-dyer of Amiens; the laborer especially; in brief, man at his trade taking possession of matter and of the world. The iconography of the thirteenth century...was evangelical, human, western and natural. It brought Christ down practically to the level of men." (9.232)

Does this not parallel our waking up to the new science today that is talking about earth as Gaia and gifting us with a new creation story and a revitalized cosmology—one that transcends every culture and religious tradition (but does not have to contradict the wisdom therein) and that can unite all humans today?

A shared ethics results from a creation story and in the twelfth century: "Even ethics came to be based on nature, whose laws are the rules of well-being and the guarantee of happiness. All of this in their view did not detract from the absolute power of God; for this nature, mistress of the universe, was the expression and 'vicar' of the Almighty, in the words of Alan of Lille." (9.233) A similar teaching is occurring today vis a vis the new cosmology of our time. In their book, *The New Universe and the Human Future: How a Shared Cosmology Could Launch a Global Society*, Nancy Ellen Abrams and Joel Primack, cosmologists of considerable renown, discuss how to translate the new cosmology into a shared ethic before humanity destroys itself and much of the rest of the Earth and its species as we know them.

4. People of Francis' time were waking up and coming into their own power, learning to trust their minds, their senses and their visions. Science helped with that insofar as awe was reawakened and with it hope and new possibilities because "that wonderment experienced by minds which...moved out of the social and intellectual immaturity of serfdom, discovered life's ordered energies, its instincts, its laws and its freedom, the rhythmic movement of the season and the recurrent life-cycles of living beings." (9.18f) At stake was nothing less than a realization of the universe as sacrament which "provided for the spirit an immediate nourishment drawn from the sacramental character of the universe; for, even before men contemplate it, the sacramental universe is filled with God." (9.35)

Instead of bearing contempt for the world, which was the basis of much of the former monastic spirituality, a new appreciation and curiosity about the world found expression, accompanied by an eagerness to discover nature rather than brush it off. "All of nature belongs to secular science, but all of nature is sacred as well. It is merely one's perspective that changes, and science and mysticism ought naturally to complement one another." (9.47)

I find this yearning to discover the universe in Francis' day to parallel the excitement one feels among people today—especially the young—when they hear the new cosmology. This means the "secular" vs. "Christian" dualism that fundamentalists set up in today's discourse (and that includes the previous two popes) is simply unacceptable. It is, to borrow your own phraseology, narcissistic and leads to ecclesiolatry or ecclesial narcissism. It is also anti-intellectual. Are any of the new sects so beloved by the past two popes in touch with today's cosmology? I doubt it. Many young people are totally turned off by such dualisms which totally reject the awe, wonder and spiritual energy behind much of today's science. It is simplistic and destructive. For the Church to follow that path is a sure trail to oblivion.

5. Another lesson to learn from the times in which Francis lived and operated and the milieu from which he emerged is the issue of economics. His vow of poverty was strikingly different from that of the monks who by the twelfth century were thoroughly embedded within the feudal system and profiting heavily from it in so many ways. "Poverty made the necessary break, for it represented both a rejection of the avarice and vanity of the new world and a liberation from the temporal security of the old regime...Thus it involved more than moral purification inspired by the good will of reformers; the twelfth century already had enough of that. It involved the shaping of an evangelical truth to a determined socio-economic form...the Poor Men of Lyon [and] the Humiliati of Lombardy...simply settled down in a different world, with which it was necessary to be in communication in order to address to it the word of God." (9.235)

The new thinkers, Francis included, sided with the critics of privilege of their day and, as Chenu insists, it was not merely an issue of personal or "moral purification" but of recognizing social/economic structures that were on the one hand profiting a few and on the other were taking advantage of many. Surely this is echoed today amid efforts to analyze and critique economic and political privilege that so drives geo-political imperial ambitions and that lies behind so much of the destruction of the earth wrought by multi-national corporations and countries who defend them. It is a poor strategy to label someone a Marxist when they only recognize that love without justice is not love but a sentimentalizing of love. Marx's ideology couldn't get him to these ideas, but rather he took them from the Jewish prophets of the Bible and people who live out such resistance do so out of devotion to the teachings of Jesus and other Biblical prophets.

Brother Pope Francis, I find you speaking clearly on this very topic on many occasions. As when you say that "Christianity condemns both Communism and wild capitalism with the same vigor," and you denounce the "flight of money to foreign countries" as a sin because it dishonors "the people that worked to generate" that wealth. (1.160) And when you say that we have to reject the "wild economic liberalism we see today" and "seek equal opportunities and rights and strive for social benefits, dignified retirement, vacation time, rest, and freedom of unions." (1.172) I like how you endorse the "shantytown priests" working in Argentina and recognize how they are actually causing transformation within the ecclesial community. I appreciate your naming Francis' charism in the following way, when you say that "he brought to Christianity an idea of poverty against the luxury, pride, vanity of the civil and ecclesiastical powers of the time" and for this reason "he changed history." (1. 231) I am on board when you warn that "human rights are not only violated by terrorism, repression, or assassination, but also by unfair economic structures that create huge inequalities." (10.88) The latest disaster in Bangladesh which took the lives of over 1000 already poorly paid workers at a clothes factory is truth of what you speak.

Francis would be speaking out about these matters also.

Given the parallels between Francis' time and revolution and ours, I want to ask: Is a renaissance possible in our day? Might the Church assist its birth? Does that invitation not constitute an adventure of the first order?

Chenu expounds on the renaissance of the twelfth century, that which gave birth to Francis your namesake. He often said that renaissance was the only one that worked in Europe because it was not top-down as was the fifteenth/sixteenth century renaissance but rather from the bottom-up—freed serfs, young people, women, artisans and workers, were all part of it. Chenu says: "'Renaissance'...literally involves new birth, new existence in all the changed conditions of times, places, and persons; it represents an initiative all the more irreducible to the ancient materials it uses because it is a spiritual initiative...a discovery hitherto unimagined will be made...it was an effect incidental to a hunger of spirit. It is within the spirit that the joyous rebirth takes place; the sources just discovered had perhaps long been accessible but had long remained unproductive for want of some spirit to breathe upon the waters." (9.3,4)

Are we capable of "discoveries hitherto unimagined," of tapping into the "hunger of spirit" of young people of our time to elicit a "joyous rebirth" born of a "spiritual initiative"? Francis' brother, theologian Leonardo Boff, praises Francis for being an "antithesis" of clericalism and of "paternalism and monarchism in the institutional structure of the Church." (3.115f.) Can we imitate Francis in this regard? Surely that is the purpose of your papacy is it not, to assist in leading the way? Is there any hope for the human race today other than such a renaissance? Instead of resistance and death, might the Church instead lead such an adventure?

5 SOME CONTENT FOR THE 'NEW EVANGELIZATION' AND REVISIONING THE SACRAMENT OF ORDINATION AND PRIESTHOOD

Dear Pope Francis:

I was struck to hear of the talk you gave prior to your election as pope when you said: "When the church does not emerge from itself to evangelize, it becomes self-referential and therefore becomes sick...The evils that, over time, occur in ecclesiastical institutions have their root in self-referentiality, a kind of theological narcissism." You criticized "a mundane church that lives within itself, of itself and for itself." You insisted that whoever became the new pope should be "a man who...helps the church to emerge from itself toward the existential outskirts."[9]   I fully concur. Let me speak in this letter to some evangelical content that the world needs today. We often hear from

---

[9] Andrea Rodriguez, "Cuba cleric: Francis criticized church at conclave," *The San Diego Union-Tribune*, March 26, 2013.

the Vatican about the need for "evangelization." But what constitutes authentic "good news" as defined by the curialists is neither convincing nor of the adventurous sort I spoke of in my last letter.

I wish to offer a modest contribution to authentic evangelization and a theological perspective and tradition that can assist you to move the Church beyond its "narcissism" that lives only "within itself, of itself and for itself" in this letter.

The most important and impactful lessons I learned from studying with Pere Chenu (it was his last year of teaching since he was 75 years old at the time) was the distinction he made between the fall/redemption spiritual tradition and the creation-centered spiritual tradition. The former is deeply anthropocentric for it begins with humanity's failures whereas the latter opens the door to a profound awareness of the sacredness of all creation. Like the first chapter of Genesis, it begins with the goodness or blessing that existence and creation are.

Having taught, written, lectured, led retreats and designed programs over the past forty-four years around the Creation Spirituality tradition I believe we have here a program that speaks to today's deepest needs: Needs of honoring the sacredness of creation and therefore acting on ecological devastation; needs of deep ecumenism since we all, Christians, Buddhists, Hindus, Muslims, Jews, Atheists etc. depend on creation for our existence and there is after all no such thing as a Roman Catholic rainforest or a Buddhist ocean or a Lutheran sun or a Baptist moon. We are in this together and a consciousness of creation (as opposed to merely religious narcissism and petty sectarianism) calls us all to be mindful and generous today in standing up to resist climate change and violence and to change our lifestyles so our species fits more fully into the rhythms of nature.

Creation Spirituality is also important today because it can help move religion away from its self-centeredness and preoccupation with power and institutions, or what you rightly call its "narcissism," to practice. Spirituality is about practice more than just sociological structures or dogmas. It is about meditation and calming the reptilian brain—and don't we all need that desperately? It is about the love and joy of life or what the mystics call the Via Positiva, the joy of living. Aquinas: "Sheer joy is God's and this demands companionship"—thus the very reason for the universe is joy. Listen to what Thomas Berry, a priest of the Passionist Order who died two years ago, and who devoted his life to learning the new science and the new cosmology said about what we now know about the universe: "The human venture depends absolutely on this quality of awe and reverence and joy in the Earth and all that lives and grows upon the Earth...In the end the universe can only be explained in terms of celebration. It is all an exuberant expression of existence itself." (2.166, 170)

Yes, the "exuberance of existence itself." Recently I acquired a puppy and while I can't judge yet how wise a decision that was at my age, this I do know: the puppy teaches the exuberance of life. Yes to the celebration of life. And do you know where this takes us? It puts us in the same camp with the goddess era because feminist archeologist Marija Gimbutas wrote that the "essence of the goddess civilization was the celebration of life." As Rabbi Heschel teaches, "praise precedes faith." To put joy of life first, to truly preach and teach the Via Positiva, would cut the umbilical cord with patriarchy that is so imperial in its goals and processes and that has manipulated our religion long enough. Thus a third contribution of Creation Spirituality is to welcome back the goddess, the divine feminine, into a culture and world that is out of balance. How will our species possibly survive if yin/yang, feminine and masculine, are not in balance in our souls and the structures we give birth to?

Science and religion do not have to be at odds. They are both about God's creation and we need scientists to tell us more about the wonders of that creation both at the macrocosmic and microcosmic levels. I was pleased that your partner in dialog, Rabbi Skorka, was also a scientist and that you once studied chemistry as a young man. A fourth gift of Creation Spirituality is a new relationship between science and spirituality. Many are the scientists today who are rediscovering the marvel and miracle and wonder and awe of the universe and assisting us to do the same. The Via Positiva indeed. It has been my privilege to enter into public dialogs with a number of scientists including the British biologist Rupert Sheldrake with whom I have authored two books. I learn so much from science and the Creation Spirituality tradition has always considered science a priority. (Hildegard wrote: "all science comes from God" and she said that our greatest gift is our gift of intellect.)

Of course the Via Positiva is not (alas!) all that life is about or that the spiritual journey is about. We also undergo the Via Negativa, as it is named in the Creation Spirituality tradition. The Via Negativa includes silence and emptying, letting go and letting be. It is also sorrow and suffering and grief. The Via Creativa is about our creativity. And the Via Transformativa is about justice and compassion, in other words, our powers of healing.

Since you have a special relationship with Jewish rabbis in Argentina I think you will enjoy the following story. After I presented these "four paths" of the creation spiritual tradition over thirty years ago at the Lutheran School of Theology at GTU in Berkeley, a man full of energy and excitement came up to me. He said he was Jewish and had done his doctorate under Gershom Scholem in his birth country of Switzerland, and Scholem, as you know, is a great scholar of Jewish mysticism. He said to me: "You are the first Christian theologian I have ever heard who deliberately rejected the three paths of purgation, illumination and union which are not Jewish and these four paths you have named today—these are Jewish! Now the dialog can begin." Also, he said, "your emphasis on Jesus and Wisdom is another bridge we have not crossed until now. That too means the interaction can begin!"

Today's New Testament scholarship agrees with the teaching I've emphasized for years on Jesus as a Wisdom teacher. We are told finally that Jesus comes from the wisdom tradition of Israel. But the wisdom tradition of Israel is the creation-centered spiritual tradition that is nature based more than book-based. Jesus was a Jewish peasant whose closeness to earth comes through in all of his parables and teachings. The lessons he draws about God come from observing nature closely. So in preaching Creation Spirituality we are indeed "returning to the Gospels." Wisdom also includes justice—she is "a friend of the prophets"—and Wisdom includes creativity (Hildegard: "There is wisdom in all creative works") and an interest in cosmology since she was "playing with God before the creation of the world."

You see, it is not enough that people "evangelize" in the name of the Church. Simply put, what are we preaching as the "good news" today? And this is where the rise of christofascism in Christianity is truly scary, for instead of preaching a balance of male and female, and justice for women, and justice toward the earth and her creatures, and the need for economic and social justice, many so-called Christians today, under the guise of falsely named "lay movements" such as Opus Dei, Communion and Liberation, the Legion of Christ, and Focolare are preaching something else. They are not preaching these gospel values at all. In no way are they returning to our Christian sources for renewal. I look in vain in the groups' writings for any hint of justice. They don't have a clue about the oldest spiritual tradition in the Bible (and beyond it), that of Creation Spirituality. Instead they are preaching a "theology" of authoritarianism that can only be summarized as "obey the pope." Indeed they are not preaching theology at all but a kind of authoritarianism covered over with pious sentimentalisms. And sentimentalism, as a fine scholar demonstrated years ago is a kind of "rancid political consciousness"—one that covers up injustice and refuses to face it. Or, as Carl Jung put it, behind the sentimental facade there always lurks violence. The SS captains of concentration camps often tortured and murdered people during the day then returned to their families in the evening when they would play Bach or Beethoven on their pianos and cry.

The Creation Spirituality tradition is also a proponent of a Cosmic Christ perspective that I wrote about in my third letter. Indeed, I like to say that authentic Christianity flies on two wings—that of the historic Jesus (who derives from the Wisdom and the prophetic traditions of Israel) and that of the Cosmic Christ. This is the understanding of the Christ that preceded the Nicene Creed of the fourth century (the time the church married the empire)—it is found in the earliest sources of Christianity, that is, in the earliest hymns and epistles such as Colossians, Philippians, and Ephesians.

"In Christ were created all things in heaven and on earth: everything visible and invisible...Before anything was created, Christ existed, and Christ holds all things in unity." (Col. 1:15-17) "God has made known to us in all wisdom and insight the mystery of the divine will, according to the divine purpose which God set forth in Christ as a plan for the fullness of time, to unite all things in Christ, things in heaven and things on earth." (Eph. 1:9-10)

Why is the Church not celebrating these hymns to the Cosmic Christ more vigorously today? After all, the tremendous new knowledge about the universe has every thinking person and especially the young abuzz with excitement. Why stick with a fourth century Christology that mirrors the philosophical battles of the Greek empire instead of returning to our sources in the New Testament? These older sources celebrate the Cosmic Christ.

It is not enough to talk about "evangelization." The *content* of evangelization is crucial. After all most of the advertising industry today is built on "evangelization," i.e., promises that buying one's product will offer salvation or healing or beauty or power. The content of true evangelization today needs to be—as it was in Francis' revolution—the Gospel values themselves, values of joy and of letting go, of creativity and responsibility, of compassion and justice. The Four Paths of Creation Spirituality lay out an ample agenda for authentic preaching of the Good News in our time—of authentic evangelization. A pope could do a lot to put such messaging into the world and to support those who do.

Since Jesus wisely reminded us that it is "by their fruits that you shall know them," I wish to speak of just two persons who have been practicing Creation Spirituality in our time. Their work, I believe, is the best indicator of the power of this tradition. The first is Bernard Amadei who told me, when he joined my Doctor of Ministry in Creation Spirituality degree program in 2002 that he was "burned out" by both academia (where he had taught engineering for twenty-seven years) and by engineering. "I don't know what's next for me," he said. Two weeks later he came to me and said, "I've gotten my soul back." He went home to the University of Colorado where he taught and he started Engineers Without Borders, an organization that now hosts over 14,000 members who go to places like Haiti and the Amazon, Africa and Afghanistan to assist people in building solar generated irrigation systems and much more—all the marvels (i.e., miracles) that engineers can do. Many of the members of EWB are young engineers who are thrilled by the opportunity to serve the poor in place of having to sell their souls to large corporations. When I ran into Bernard last year, who now works at the United Nations, he told me "it all began with my two weeks at the University of Creation Spirituality."

With conversions like these, Creation Spirituality might even be able to invigorate cardinals and ecclesial bureaucrats who need a retreat with a new direction in life. I am happy to offer my services to you to retrain the Curia in a theology that matters and that relates to our Gospel origins of Christianity; that is, to the wisdom or Creation Spirituality tradition.

Another graduate of our program was Sister Dorothy Stang, a sister of Notre Dame de Namur from the state of Ohio in the United States. Sister Dorothy was 73 years old and living and working in the Amazon Rainforest in Brazil when she was gunned down on February 12, 2005 by three gunmen hired by plantation owners who resented her work among the poor that focused on developing sustainable farming and defending the Amazon from slash-and-burn agriculture. Cattle ranchers and illegal logging corporations were outraged by her effort. As she encountered her murderers on a walk along a muddy road, she pulled out her Bible and read three beatitudes to them: "Blessed are the poor in spirit, blessed are those who hunger and thirst for justice, blessed are the peacemakers." They shot her six times. Before her funeral in Anapu, Brazil, one of the poor farmers with whom she worked said: "We are not going to bury Dorothy; we are going to plant her."

Sister Dorothy died a martyr; she died like the martyrs of the early church, planting seeds of justice and compassion toward the earth and toward future generations. We are very proud of her. When she returned to Brazil after finishing her master's degree with us in 1992 she wrote every month and told us that her studies and practices in Creation Spirituality kept her going, committed as ever to her people, despite the death threats she continued to receive. She could have left Brazil but she chose instead to stay. "I don't want to flee," she said, "nor do I want to abandon the battle of these farmers who live without any protection in the forest. They have the sacrosanct right to aspire to a better life on land where they can live and work with dignity while respecting the environment." Sister Dorothy knew about the Via Transformativa and lived it to the end.[10]

You are from South America, Pope Francis. Now you live in Rome and are Bishop of Rome. You know and I know the great danger in imagining that the time of the martyrs is only a nostalgic memory to be conjured up while touring catacombs or ancient churches of Rome with relics of old saints amidst bus-loads of tourists. You know and I know that Sister Dorothy's story is by no means unique in our time. Thousands of church workers from Oscar Romero to Sister Dorothy to many others—priests, sisters

---

[10] A fine book of Sister Dorothy's story has already been published. See Binka Le Breton, *The Greatest Gift: The Courageous Life and Martyrdom of Sister Dorothy Stang* (New York: Doubleday, 2007).

and lay people—have sacrificed their lives for social justice and eco justice all across the Americas. The blood of these martyrs must not be in vain. They have stood up to the empires of our day whether that of the CIA or of multi-national corporations and have given the greatest gift a person can give so that others may live. Their courage matches that of the victims fed to the lions by the Empire in the coliseum centuries ago.

The fact that a sister trained in Creation Spirituality found that teaching to be supportive of her generous vocation is an obvious sign that the recovery of that tradition in our time is of great importance. It builds courage even as it creates a useful and profound value system. I was deeply touched to learn from one of Sister Dorothy's brothers that when he traveled to Brazil after she was murdered he found next to her bed my books on Creation Spirituality, all read and marked up. I tell you this because it is time that Rome beefed up its theological message. All evangelism is not equal. Preach the Gospel. Not neo-fascist propaganda.

Pope Francis, all over the world people are feeling embarrassed to call themselves Catholic. The anti-intellectual sects that are masquerading as lay movements that I referred to earlier have been, for the past thirty five years, receiving the Vatican's utmost promotion. Furthermore, it is from their ranks that countless bishops and cardinals of the Church have been appointed during the past two papacies. This will not do. They are not trained in a Gospel spirituality. Isn't it an embarrassment to you, as a Jesuit, to know that the Church is being run by anti-intellectuals, or what one Brazilian bishop called "neurotics for orthodoxy"? Being a Jesuit you belong to a proud intellectual tradition—isn't it time that a respect for theologians and what they do be returned to the Church? Isn't it time to end the Inquisition just as the Second

Vatican Council ended the Index of Forbidden Books? Isn't it time to support, rather than interfere with, those theological movements that are returning us to the basic message of the Gospels? Isn't this what Francis was all about?

We have already seen how a renewed sense of cosmology, our place in the universe and the 13.8 billion year journey that has birthed our species into the cosmos, can set the stage for an adventure once again. The cosmos is the primary sacrament and all the other sacraments derive their power and energy from that reality. As Francis knew, we live in a sacramental universe and it is in this holy context that we need to reset our understanding and preaching of our faith. My brother Dominican Father Edward Schillibeeckx wrote a powerful and influential book some forty years ago entitled *Christ the Sacrament of the Encounter with God* that has influenced many. Yes, the Cosmic Christ and the Sacraments go together. In the context of the Cosmic Christ we can and ought to take another look at the Sacraments of the Church.

Let us discuss just one of those sacraments, that of ordination or priesthood. Lately there has been considerable discussion among historians that suggests there was no priesthood in the Christian body until the second century. It is true that all human gatherings need some kind of leadership, even if it means passing the role around among the membersor periodically adjusting it. So no doubt the priesthood developed in the second century in response to those universal sociological needs. Jesus chose his disciples and trained them in his teachings so that they could carry them on but the myth that he 'ordained' them or established priesthood is, strictly speaking, a later fabrication. It might be useful for the establishment of a kind of mythological order, but it is not historically based.

Your namesake himself fiercely resisted the priesthood for himself and his band of followers. One of his greatest fears was that his order would become clericalized. I am pleased to note that you too are sensitive about the issue of clericalization and applaud how you have spoken out against it calling clericalism "a distortion of religion" and insisting that "the Catholic Church is the entire People of God, including priests" and demanding that priests listen to their community instead of saying "I am the boss here" and thus falling "into clericalism." (1.138)

We live in a time of a great dearth of priestly "vocations" in Europe, North America as well as South America also. Some people wring their hands and say unhelpfully "this is the end of the Church" because so few sacraments are available to people and this is the "triumph of secularism." Others say selfishly "it is good—we can be a smaller and more orthodox church." Others more helpfully and less selfishly say, "ordain women and let married people be priests and the problem is solved." While I am in agreement somewhat with the latter, I also offer a deeper critique of the sacrament.

I have proposed that the basic meaning of priesthood, its archetypal power, is as a midwife of grace. For me, that is what the priesthood is all about. We need midwives of grace, surely we do. If a priest is essentially not one anointed by Jesus (as modern scholarship maintains), nevertheless the power of the archetype is still among us. I propose that if anyone among us is doing good work, work that qualifies as a midwife of grace, then that person is a priest.

Given that understanding of priesthood, we are not so short of priests after all. Doctors and business people, artists and teachers, therapists and social workers, carpenters and car repair specialists, farmers and journalists, inventors and policemen and women, nurses and builders and engineers and bankers who are bringing grace into the world are priests. Luther talked about the "priesthood of all believers" but I am speaking of the "priesthood of all workers." What follows from this?

First, that we must radically change our education of all these workers to encompass instruction in their mystical and prophetic journeys. Such people need instruction in the experiences of grace they rarely received in their professional training. They need to get more in touch with their mystical selves and the prophetic dimensions of their work—how can they most effectively interfere? How can they help turn their profession into an instrument of justice-making and healing? Is this possible, to re-educate such persons? Indeed it is.

That is what my University of Creation Spirituality did for nine years and we did it most successfully. It is not that difficult to bring the mystic and prophet alive again in people and especially in their professional work. Most people are more than aware that their greatest impact— other than parenting—on culture and history will be the work they do in the world. Work is a sacrament. That is what I am saying. We have every right and need to 'anoint' people in their chosen professions and vocations once they have demonstrated they can assist the resacralization of their profession and are willing to make the sacrifices necessary to bring that about. I have proof from literally hundreds of our graduates that this revisioning of 'seminary training' is possible. That is why our program offered a Doctor of Ministry degree and not a Ph.D.— because spirituality is a pastoral thing, a practical thing, a thing we must put into practice.

A second consequence of reimagining the Sacrament

of Ordination has to do with the religious or clerical priesthood as we know it. You yourself have spoken out against clericalism and clerical attitudes. But what can we do about that disease? One thing we can do is to invite this 'army' of other priests, those from our various professions that I refer to above, to lead in preaching and teaching and overseeing Sacramental ministries. Some of these will be called to that, others will not.

We can also retrain the clergy we have and completely redo the training new clergy receive. The latter ought to be thrown in with those who constitute the broader meaning of priesthood I allude to above—let them learn of the mystical and prophetic paths elbow-to-elbow and shoulder-to-shoulder with the artists, therapists, social workers, teachers, activists and others who are learning it. Do away with the hothouse atmosphere of make-believe clerical worlds. We no longer need seminaries as such. Community living? Yes. And working with the poor and not just others involved in formal education? Yes.

Again, we have proven over many years the deep and lasting effectiveness of a spiritual training in the creation spiritual tradition, one that incorporates Scripture and theology, social change and psychology, art as meditation and other forms of meditation that leaders can share with their communities. I am happy to give this model of pedagogy away and teach it to others so that more and more people can be trained in it.

A third dimension to awakening priesthood in our time is to listen to the wisdom of the late Father Thomas Berry, who said we need fewer priests and fewer professors and more shamans. The vocation of shamanism—that oldest of all midwiferies of grace—is coming back on our time and for obvious reasons. The shaman is a link between this world and other worlds and the shaman is connected to Mother Earth and her creatures in an especially powerful and embodied way. Francis himself was deeply shamanistic. The shaman has died to self and resurrected to serve others. No wonder so many young people are feeling called to that kind of service today rather than the clerical priesthood. Mother Earth is doing the calling. It is clear the Jesus himself embodied many shamanistic characteristics including his retreat to the desert to wrestle with spirits and be among the wild animals of the wilderness after his baptism (Mark 1), his calming of the waters, his deep relationship with nature, his many wilderness retreats, his apprenticing with John the Baptist in the desert as an adolescent—all this adds more points to his shamansitic side, a dimension that has been largely absent in our academically oriented seminary training.

I think it is time to shut down all seminaries that do not heed the teaching of Thomas Aquinas that "revelation comes in two volumes, the Bible and nature." If we are not training religious leaders about the revelation of nature but only about the Bible book we are inviting complete irrelevance. Science teaches us about nature and we ought to be honoring the wisdom that is there and incorporating the mysticism of science into our curricula. The same is true of indigenous wisdom for the ancient peoples, who have never lost their respect for and reverence for our sacred relationship to the earth and her creatures. Like Francis himself! And let us be honest—Francis never attended a seminary. Could he have kept his soul intact, his nature-fed experience of the Cosmic Christ if he had attended a seminary? Jesus also never attended a seminary. My guess is that both would have been expelled for being too right-brained, too mystical, too eager to challenge culture and religion.

We know that seminaries were established as part of

the counter-reformation because so many clergy at the time were functionally illiterate. Surely that era has passed. Do we need seminaries that teach so narrow a literacy and become irrelevant educational institutions? Why not have future religious leaders trained side by side with other midwives of grace? Such an approach would not only make for a fuller intellectual life but would offer the distinct advantage of advancing a more mature moral and psychological development so as to resist addictions to power, whether ecclesial, sexual or interpersonal.

Still another implication of this reinvented sense of the priesthood is that, given its broader context and setting, the gender wars over whether women can be ordained pretty much disappear. Of course, women are an integral part of all the professions I have listed. Women have experienced profound callings to lead and to serve, including in positions such as presidents and prime ministers all over the world, including in your native country of Argentina, and her neighboring Brazil. If Jesus did not ordain anyone (and he didn't), then surely there is no argument that "Jesus only ordained men" which is the only—and utterly lame—argument for gender exclusion. If you want to end clericalism overnight, the surest and fastest way is to open the priesthood to women. All of them.

Biblical scholars today are instructing us that leadership roles in the first generation of the Christ movement were by no means restricted to men. Indeed, it was the opening to women and their wisdom that constituted one of the most revolutionary dimensions to the person and teaching of Jesus. Even Paul talks about the support he received from women leaders. Thus the notion that women should be excluded from leadership is traceable to only one place: the fear in the heart of men, and gatherings of men that they will somehow be eclipsed by women. I have listened to women talking about their vocation for the past forty- three years and it is undeniable that women too are called to minister and always have been.

Indeed, the renowned and respected New Testament scholar Bruce Chilton, in his brilliant book on Mary Magdalene, proposes that Jesus bequeathed his anointing ministry to Mary Magdalene (the town of Magdalena he points out was famous in Israel for producing women healers) and thus it can accurately be said that the entire Sacramental tradition of the Church in a profound sense actually owes its inspiration and origin to a woman. If we want to renew the Sacraments today how can we possibly do so without including women in leadership once again?

Not only were Jesus' actions and relationships with women a breakthrough and scandal in his day, but Francis too provides ample witness to the need for the balance of female energies in ministry—his brilliant poem "Brother Sun and Sister Moon" navigates back and forth between the masculine and the feminine, the yin and the yang. His poem is a true window into the soul of your namesake. In his relationship with Clare, twelve years his junior and a strong leader in her own right, we have concrete evidence that gender balance contributed to church reformation. Francis didn't want Claire confined to a cloister, but rather preaching alongside his band of brothers. Alas, due to church intransigence of the time, that was not to be until the Franciscan third order and what we call today "Franciscan sisters," was established long after Francis' death.

Indeed, Thomas of Celano's two biographies of Francis suffered, in the words of one historian, because Thomas was in fact a "church propagandist" swimming in a "powerful current of bigotry" toward women. This is clear because he fails to give any account of Francis' role in establishing Clare and her sisters as his Second Order in San Damiano, but even more so because his second biography of Francis portrays him as a misogynist. Such bigotry and misogyny was true of ecclesial circles in Thomas' time and it shows itself today in the highest levels of the Catholic Church.

But the important lesson remains. Francis was a trumpet for the Sacred Feminine, a spirit which was everywhere in the air following the Gothic revolution of the twelfth century, which overturned centuries of masculine architecture and set forward a more inclusive sociological reality that is found in the 80 some cathedrals built in this era, each one dedicated to the goddess—Notre Dame de Paris, Notre Dame de Chartres, Notre Dame de Lyon, etc. Francis celebrated and promoted the amazing accomplishments of Clare along with her sister Catherine, who took the name "Agnes" and joined her community even after being violently attacked by relatives for daring to do so. Francis made sure that his brothers assisted them in every way possible whether begging food, collecting fuel, or providing extra space as their numbers grew. And grow they did, as the sisters Clare attracted numbered over fifty at San Damiano alone and they would run into hundreds, including royalty and half a dozen saints. Today it is nearly impossible to find a trace of Francis' respect for strong women among our fearful clerics who ignore these gifts to their own detriment.

I was encouraged to see you invoke in your book of dialogs the wisdom and strength of your grandmother and cite a woman playwright, Nini Marshall. Hopefully you will have an experience of women theologians as well. I have profited deeply from reading them and learning from them in numerous situations.

I am encouraged by your actions on Holy Thursday, your first as pope, when you washed the feet of young people in jail, some of whom were women. But your attention to these women incited the fury of clerics and others who have practiced their sexism with impunity the past thirty five years. There have been Vatican- sponsored attacks on women, such as the current investigations of American sisters like Sister Dorothy Stang who have been living out the principles and values of Vatican II and the gospels for decades. We must meditate on why there was such a furious response to your symbolic action of washing the feet of women prisoners, for the reason is obvious: You have dared to touch the scab of sexism in the Church and in the clerical church in particular. I congratulate you for this Francis-like action (indeed Jesus-like) for it is the beginning of much else that can be done.

The sharing of the Eucharist, which is part of the priestly role, takes on ever deeper and more cosmic meaning in a theology of the Cosmic Christ. Given what we know about the universe today including its 13.8 billion year history and its size of hundreds of billions of galaxies each with hundreds of millions of stars, it is nothing short of awe-inspiring to imagine that we each and together can eat, digest and be nourished by the food of the universe itself. By eating and drinking the body and life force of the Cosmic Christ we are connecting to the entire universe and its amazing history. We are not alone. We are in this together. Communion is real—communion with all the beings and all the history and all the liveliness and creativity and expansion taking place in the universe.

Furthermore, it is hard to imagine anything more intimate or more erotic than eating. And we do that when we take the Eucharist which is after all a big Thank You (since *eucharistein* means thank you in Greek). Gratitude and reverence emerge from such a sharing. And still more sharing as the communities of which we are a part and with whom we share this meal are also blessed by the same divine food and drink.

The question remains: Can the Church renew its Sacramental charism? Surely not within the confines of a clerical system that is more bent on preserving its privileges than on midwifing grace. And not under the direction of the negative senex, that is of old people running old institutions in old patterns to serve old ways.

What is fresh and dynamic and healing about a sacramental tradition can be rediscovered by a new generation working with elders who know that tradition. Such a task can be a mighty adventure indeed. But it will take work and it will take creativity and it will take some respect for the chaos that accompanies all creativity, a respect Francis surely had. Law and order, more canon laws and canon lawyers, with their lists of rules and do's and don'ts that are so remote from the lives of people are an obstacle to a functioning priesthood and to the renewal that Spirit and Grace are eager to bring about.

6 SMALL COMMUNITIES

Dear Pope Francis:

Many Catholics, following the principle of *sensus fidelium*, have not been waiting around for permission from on high to practice their priesthood. They have formed small communities in many parts of the world and certainly in North America. This is especially true of the older generations. I was pleased to see you endorse such gatherings when you said the following to Rabbi Skorka: "That is a key, the trend toward a small community as a place of religious belonging. It responds to a need for identity, not only a religious identity, but also a cultural identity...The origin of Christianity was 'parochial...they later organized into small communities." (1.227) You are right! I appreciate when you say that you are "in favor" of smaller communities and that "instead of there being hierarchical mega-institutions, the idea is to return to smaller congregations that nurture their own spirituality." (1.224f)

I equally appreciate the ecclesiology you articulate when you say: "Usually in journalism when they say 'The

Church' they refer to the bishops, the priests, the hierarchy; but the Church is the entire People of God." (1.209) I hasten to add, however, that many journalists get their definition of church from media 'experts' and curial cardinals supposedly speaking in the pope's name.

Recently I devised a simple survey which I have been distributing to members of various communities around my country and I want to share some of the findings with you. These are not people who hate the Church but people who, like Jesus and Francis, love it enough to move beyond its legalisms and its "mega-institutions" to carry out the spirit and the mission of the Gospel as the Spirit speaks to them. Much like Francis, they hear Christ saying, "rebuild my church" and never imagine that only popes are called to that task. So they have acted.

Following are some women and men of our—yours and mine—generation, reporting about their participation in these small communities. I think it is very important that we be good listeners and hear them out, for there is much wisdom that bubbles up from these people—as you put it, "sometimes it's more comfortable to play deaf, put on the Walkman and not listen to anyone." Here is our chance to listen.

Why are you in a small community? What drew you?

"I believe that this form of community resembles the early church better than the large parishes...large churches...large conformity issues. Though I respect the long traditions of the Church I think we have lost direction and the Church shows a distinct power struggle and disrespect for the contribution of women to the church." (77 yo female)

"A need to be with like-minded people and as a balance to the dogma of church hierarchy." (75 yo female)

"We attend a weekly home group in someone's house and I feel I get more from that than the big church. I get to be able to speak and we work things out as a group, you know the details of faith, bible, etc. I don't like the big church preaching something I don't agree with like gay marriage, which I support, and I'm supposed to just sit back passively and listen." (56 yo female)

"The control factor in the church hierarchy, patriarchy, misogyny, criminality and hypocrisy with a big dash of rudeness thrown in made the whole Roman Catholic experience a toxic spiritual cesspool. We like the informality and the non-judgmental way we can question and explore our faith." (59 yo male)

"No power structures.
No one-person control.
Simplicity.
Simple communication.
As our Founder puts it—'The Privilege of Love.'" (male)

"Seeking to offer relevant and interactive experiences that other religious communities were not offering for younger people. Our young people have an active role and lead the worship." (33 yo male)

"We were grumbling about something else that the Church and/or our diocese was doing that we disagreed with...lack of accountability for the many priest molestations as just one of many. We kept saying things like: "What happened to Vatican II?" We even called ourselves 'Disgruntled Catholics of Sonoma County'! Enough negativity, we thought, let's take our Church back!

We had our first Eucharistic Liturgy—no one is ordained and several members are considered presiders. We are an inclusive community, women, men, straight, gay, Catholic and non-Catholic. We all call upon our baptismal priesthood for our 'authority.'" (79 yo male)

"Have felt the need for deeper involvement in a faith community for many years. Really want to make a difference in terms of inclusivity (of women, of gay and lesbian couples, of divorced persons, openness to persons of other faiths). Reform of the Church from within is a waste of precious time and energy!" (66 yo female)

"More and more of the words I heard coming from the pulpit did not include me, even though I was told—by those same priests—that they did. I spent many a mass crying afterward and trying to figure out why. It seemed so unreal—and I had no idea why the torrent of tears was coming out of me! For a time I started taking notes in mass to try and figure out what was triggering my emotions. It was so frustrating! Finally, I just left. There were other ways I could carry on my FAITH (no religion, mind you, but faith which to me is more important) and I'm so glad I started attending the small faith groups! What a difference it has made. I feel healthier!" (52 yo female)

"Wanting to be part of a sacramental church but not a larger institutional church." (female)

"Intimacy and personal invitation, depth of silence and relationships, not finding that intimacy in a larger institution." (58 yo female)

"Our community is an inclusive environment where all are welcome as in the teachings of Jesus the Christ. A feeling of community you do not find in a larger parish or community. And of course the Women priests and deacons drew me...Recruitment is slow. I believe if more Catholics knew about this community and it was sanctioned by the Vatican we would not have any trouble recruiting members...I can practice my religion in a safe inviting environment where I feel welcome. I do not get this at the conventional churches...My partner has left the church due to the treatment of homosexuals." (56 yo woman)

"What drew me to this community was that I 'couldn't take it anymore' with the Institutional Roman Catholic Church moving backward, taking back the ground gained by Vatican II, the sad theologies denying women as equals, and the 'top down' structure of the Church. We look to having a more 'circular leadership,' and to being an inclusive, open, affirming community." (79 yo woman)

"Our presider can be an ordained catholic woman priest or someone from the community...I am drawn to this community because the traditional catholic church is exclusive, authoritarian, and not apart of today's world. For me, the Vatican does not manifest the Love that is Jesus. I need inclusiveness, openness, a community that lives Love, and practices Creation theology. I need to focus on people, their gifts and their needs, not on cathedrals and medieval clothes....When community gathers, I experience the God presence through other folks. How wonderful!" (79 yo male)

"What drew me to our small community was that I had been looking for a community of inclusion (interfaith), intelligence and a heartfelt sense of the teachings of Jesus along with the other great teachers of the world

"All my life (I am 81) I have searched out community." (81 yo female)

"The Illuminators is a newly formed spiritually based group of creative people that meet quarterly during the year to revive and keep alive the tradition of ancient manuscript illumination, using contemporary design and art interpretation. The focus of this spiritual group is, 'Pray, create, illuminate.' The nature of the creative process encourages small community as creating art is such a personal and individual process!" (female)

"Ours is a Catholic Worker community with the name of Casa Esther...Casa Esther is rather small in its central setting but reaches out to many, with a special focus on the Spanish speaking immigrants." (male)

"Friendly, caring people, supportive, originally anger and disappointment in institutional church, now that is not so important." (69 yo female)

"I needed something beyond what the Vatican II Church was providing. Anger, frustration, sadness, were all part of my leaving it. I feel/believe I was led by the Divine to "The More"; a closer union with a Spirit that is the One." (71 yo female)

"Anger, pain and disappointment after our progressive, Vatican II parish, was destroyed by our bishop for no good reasons." (58 yo female)

"I have many long term relationships with former religious in the group. We tend to be on the same page about reforms and can't wait around for the church." (73 yo female)

"Participation in the small community offers more spiritual fulfillment than anger towards the church." (69 yo female)

"Disgust with the deadly boring nature of the regular Sunday Mass. Desire for a New Church with meaningful liturgies which include women priests, married priests, gays, and young people." (62 yo female)

"That is what our Sunday morning Mass is missing. Our lives and culture is just too complicated and stressful to walk in and out of Church and hope to be renewed for the week. We need one on one dialogue and bondedness in a small spiritual community like I have experienced." (female)

"What drew me to my small Community was the interfaith component. The ability to study in a place where all ideas were welcomed and valued and looked at as part of the whole...Everyone has a voice and is valued...How to become leaders without being bullies is a big thing." (55 yo male)

"The small community makes the word of God more relevant. It does not lean on liturgy but uses a variety of sources to bring meaning to life and this world we live in." (69 yo female)

"What drew me was more disgust than anger...lack of nourishment, inability to accept new language which, for me, excludes people, and my faith community are lively people all searching and sharing in a safe environment...very welcoming and inclusive." (71 yo female)

"Organized religion does not delve deeply into the mystical union and the Cosmic Christ. I need more than I have so far found in any church. They mostly seem focused on getting your money, controlling your opinions and getting you to work. They ignore recent scholarship and hold to the old ways before critical think and deeper understanding came into play. I am a seeker wishing to be as spiritually aware and awake as I possibly can." (73 yo female)

"Politics and spirituality are intertwined because the direction in which you want to see society evolve is based on your spiritual longing and understanding. Revelation didn't end 2000 years ago. It is in every face. The greatest Holy Book is the universe itself and it continues to reveal its truths through our amazingly wonderful but dying planet. I was unable to find local Catholic or even non-Catholics who share this view, and I felt so alone though I know I am never really alone...I did a lot of searching and feel fortunate to have found the Unitarian Universalists." (female)

"Our small community reflects the inclusiveness lived by Jesus. Everyone is welcome at the table. Homilies are preached by both our pastor and assistant pastor as well as members of the community. Our focus is on a more contemporary theology that stresses peace and justice acted out in the community at large. Almost everyone works at or volunteers for an NGO."

"I was attracted to the community by the feminine vision of our pastor. There is nothing resembling hierarchy in our community. Everyone is focused on spiritual growth. We...attend retreats given by leaders in their fields. Centering prayer is encouraged as is Lectio Divina. The stress is on the divinity within, the Christ Consciousness that permeates all rather than Original Sin and guilt. How refreshing and how life giving is that!" (74 yo woman)

What have the spiritual benefits been for you?

"The spiritual benefits have been amazing! We can have the best discussions about philosophy and theology!

We sing and meditate together and I have discovered that UU's love poetry! That was a selling point for me. Poetry and creativity in general is the path toward spiritual awakening. The 'Creative right Brain' flourishes there." (female)

"People have wept at the spirit of peace and well-being We are still much like shipwrecked passengers in a life boat. Delighted we are alive and still feeling the spirit with us, but still in shock and fearful as to where the current may lead us; into Terra Incognita, probably, but certainly not back to the sinking ship!" (59 yo male)

"These people know me in my fullness, they truly know my song when I've forgotten it and do not believe my despair when I feel discouraged. They know me in all my life's journey. They are not afraid for me. They encourage me and I in turn encourage them...We seem to be able to tap into a stream that is deeper than 'organized' religious dogma. It is the spiritual stream of deep wisdom that flows through all the faith traditions." (70 yo female)

"Today we would call it SACRED CIRCLES...where all share their weekly story—their joys, hurts, pains, etc. and who they are transformed by the experience. This process bonded us together more than anything! We are emotionally closer together than some biological families...Unconditional love was the glue that kept us together. I can honestly say that this Community gave me more Spiritual sustenance than my religious community at this time...Our sharing went on for hours interspersed with prayer. I look back on this as PURE GIFT!!!" (female)

"The benefits of a small group are huge. We have good friendship & care for each other. I was ill recently and several members took me to doctors. We in turn love helping the others and it's easy to branch out into helping the community once you have a core group established...It's harder to make real friends without small groups." (from UK)

"I am growing spiritually due to the community and sharing life with each other. I find myself wanting to be more involved in people's lives due to this involvement with this smaller community."

"Our charter encourages care of the land, honors diversity, revels in the creativity of poetry and artists, values the voice of the marginalized and respects the ancient wisdom of earth centered cultures." (75 yo female)

"It helps me think...draws me to be a better person, and not through enforced guilt! I can ask questions:'Well, why is that?' or Can anyone help me/us understand?' or 'That was beautiful. Thank you for sharing.'"

"Silence, a place for deepening, social activism (housing, poverty, addictions)." (58 yo female)

"Enables me to grow spiritually, sharing love, joy and sorrow. It helps me keep on." (82 yo female)

"I like the readings the group has each time—since different people prepare the service each time we get many different ideas and themes that we share—keeps it diverse and enjoyable. It helps nourish my soul to be with people who think about their spirituality and are on a journey. Small Faith Communities that reach out to the wider community with service are an ideal way to build compassion one person at a time and to connect us all." (69 yo female)

"Concentration on spirituality rather than dogma has helped to deepen my mystical experience." (female)

"Spiritually, I experience New Life, a closer awareness of and participating in the Spirit's presence. I feel 'at home' with the members and experience spiritual healing among them. Gone are the Rules and Regulations!! I think it feels like the early Christians must have felt: something New is happening!! There is a Wonder and Awe in the coming together and celebrating as we do. And opening of heart, soul and mind and awareness that we are called to this, to share it with others." (79 yo female)

"We discuss the readings and all have thoughts that we share...It is adult education which I found lacking in my church community for years. I found that just 'Pray, Pay and Obey' was getting old."

"I am drawn by the opportunity to ask questions and hear different opinions and ideas from people well educated in areas of religion and spirituality, the opportunity to experience different liturgies centered in the gospels and open to the freedom of ideas and talents of all members of the community. Opportunities to learn through documentaries, lectures, books, and a focus on social justice." (58 yo female)

"Support. Understanding. Authentic and meaningful spiritual inquiry. Fun and laughter. Deep emotional and spiritual sharing." (66 yo female)

"For sure I am being supported spiritually and also am a deeper spiritual activist because of my small community."

"I am supported by intellectual, spiritual fellowship with book reading with non-Vatican and pre-Constantinian Catholics. Thich Nhat Hahn makes me more of a mystic." (64 yo male)

"We spend time in group meditation and do lots of

sharing in small groups and the larger groups." (71 yo female)

"We have awesome discussions which, by the way, can never take place within the larger church setting. We meet in each other's homes and bring food, so there are no expenses. We collect funds for charities and also do charitable works in the community." (69 yo female)

"My Friends support me in every way I can think of. They listen when I am struggling spiritually and when I am joyful. Steadfast is the word. Silence. Deep talk. Sharing life and death." (60 yo female)

"We like the discussions and inspirations we receive from each other in the God-centered atmosphere of the home, much like the early church. We don't worry about all the negative messages about abortion, anti-women, anti-gay, etc. that surround the brick and mortar buildings." (69 yo female)

"We rent the parish hall of an Episcopal Church...Most of our offerings go to support local, national or global charities."

"I prefer the small intentional community and the ritual that we share. It feeds me in a way that traditional worship does not. I think that is because we are all part of it. Rather than following along with something that the Vatican has dictated, and a priest administers. I had already begun a contemplative prayer practice prior to November, 2011. I believe that helped me follow the Spirit in starting this group." (64 yo female)

"The spiritual benefits of 'The Illuminators' for each participant include: The process, an opportunity for meditation/visualization/reflection on the presence of the

Divine within each of us, a non-verbal engagement with the Soul Self, to support and validate the creative spiritual process in others, understanding of the intimate connection between spirituality and creativity...This is an amazing community! We have taken the identity of "mystic" to a wonderful creative level! The hope is that we reach many who are in search of spiritual experience through the creative process and validation of our innate ability to create!" (female)

"We are 'spiritized' daily stemming from the ministry we perform. There is a profound sense of assurance that we are doing our level best to measuring up to Mt. 25 which compels us to feed the hungry, visit the sick and imprisoned and welcome the alien. Casa Esther, as it gradually becomes more known as a center for being Christ for the poor, is being recognized as source of inspiration to many others in the wider community. The compliments that come our way are received in a most humble fashion. We could do more...We focus on training our young Hispanics in the methods of community organizing, and have given this youth group the name LUNA." (male)

"The spiritual benefits of our community come from being part of a group of sincere, warm, welcoming beings moving towards wholeness. I see the heart and spirit of our small congregation which opens me up to being more grounded in my own heart and love of Jesus...I love the idea of home churches as in the days of Paul." (60 yo female)

"I work as a hospital chaplain, challenging spiritually exhausting work at times. I need to worship where my spirit is renewed and refreshed so I can continue to pour my energy and support into my work...The message of my small community is LOVE, support, example. We are

RESPECTED by the small community co-pastors not made to feel less than or not as good as the priest. I am deeply grateful to God for the generosity of our co-pastors in their giving of their lives to this ministry. Without it I would be lost...I am saved and supported to give my energies to God's people every day by their love and support each week." (68 yo female)

"Participation in this community deepens and expands my spirituality. It feeds me in ways that I did not know were possible. I am encouraged by this community to go deeper in prayer and in relationship with God, to open myself to a greater degree, to trust in God but also other people." (51 yo female)

What are your attitudes toward the Institutional Church?

"It's all so irrational and so unChrist-like. The church's man-made rules have driven the faithful away." (69 yo female)

"I believe that small communities will eventually replace the outmoded hierarchical model of Church." (66 yo female)

"I do not attend liturgies (other than funerals and weddings) in the traditional church. The liturgies seem very exclusive and the homilies not at all challenging but I am supportive of those for whom it works. I think we have to be accepting of where people are on their faith journey...In our community we have amazing liturgies and great preaching fill me. The preaching is shared by about six people and they are about current happenings in our life applied to the scripture...The community has retreat days and we do lectio and meditation often when we are together...We are a welcoming, inclusive community where everyone, no matter where they are on their spiritual journey are welcome at the table. We work very hard at being inclusive in our language, homilies and newsletter.." (81 yo woman)

"I often attend the Saturday Mass with my wife. Though I try I really don't get much nourishment. It feels like we are receiving pablum. As I look around during the service I don't think people are being nourished spiritually. It just isn't working and the new translations are hindering rather than helping. There is no opportunity for people to interact with the Scriptural texts or to share their insights into the scriptures." (male)

"I'VE HAD IT! For the church to deny any acknowledgment that priests might be abusers, as well as to cover up this abuse, is to me a travesty and SIN of the highest accord! And for the Pope to voice that denial AND THEN SAY that women's ordination is a heresy and a sin...that homosexuality is a sin...that nun's work around injustice, kindness, peace, equality and fairness is 'against the church' and a sin...what lies! What arrogance! Killing innocence, kindness and joy just can't be the way of God! I cannot bear it!" (52 yo female)

"I don't believe in a God of damnation and fear. I have learned that God is love and forgiving." (73 yo woman)

"This (smaller community) could be done as part of the institutional church, I hear of it in some other Christian churches." (69 yo female)

"The good old boy's club sent me packing." (68 yo female)

"I don't find much spiritual support from the pulpit, the pulpit is primarily focused on correct behavior including morals, how I treat others, serving others, and justice issues. There is very little spiritual formation from the pulpit." (57 yo female)

"The archdiocese continues to return to old ways and forms of prayer which are NOT supportive to me or to others, changing the language and readings instead of tending to the people's needs is a good example. It seems the RC church is more interested in CONTROLLING people than supporting them." (68 yo female)

"As a former practicing Catholic, I am keenly aware of the number of people who are former Catholics who see the church as either an obstacle or irrelevant to the social and ecological issues of our time." (55 yo male)

"While it is often easier to just leave, I believe that the Church (as the People of God) is worth fighting for. Too many people have been hurt and continue to be hurt by the authority structure and a warped model of priesthood. We all deserve better. We need to be witnessing to a God of Love, ever generous, ever expanding." (51 yo female)

"I'm beyond it. I don't think of it much. Gave it significant attention for the first 60 years of my life, have grown past a need for it." (66 yo female)

"Only interested in their own initiatives. Too big to succeed...I always felt, from a young age, that the church had misinterpreted Christ's teachings." (66 yo female)

"We take the priesthood of the laity seriously...We feel that the (institutional) church has left us, rather than our leaving it. The "Church" seems to be mired in the 16th Century and deliberately ignoring Vatican II. Imagine where we could be now if the last 50 years had been spent developing Vatican II's ideas." (72 yo male)

"Politics has kept me out of roles unfairly as a woman."

"Our small community also includes several married priests and their wives. Such a shame that the formal church excludes these magnificent men, while complaining about the shortage of priests."

"I'm probably one foot in and one foot out but I don't give it up easily. But I do feel beyond organized religion. Our group is very interfaith—we have morphed from Catholics only to Christian to others including Eastern traditions."

"I am beyond it. The Catholic Church's core teachings are still valuable for me (love, forgiveness, compassion, creativity, joy) but the institution of the church is not appealing to my needs nor wants. I do not feel an opportunity for personal growth in the repressive environment (we are all born sinners and we have to repent to be worthy and only the church can provide this to us, etc.)." (60 yo male)

"Don't attend but hate to leave for good. My entire family are staunch Catholics but I think all question the men at the top. Sex abuse by priests but more so the hiding of it by bishops and higher. Our Bishop Braxton and his misuse of funds meant for the poor on other things, his yearly vacations in Europe and his narcissistic attitude."

"My husband often goes to church but then complains about how irrelevant it is. I never attend mass anymore." (69 yo female)

"What the Church preaches/teaches/is no longer relevant to me. I do not believe the Creed or the whole redemption theology thing anymore. We do feel a connection with the early followers of Jesus who simply met in their homes and shared what might have been important to them as they tried to live kind, peace-filled lives." (71 yo female)

"I worked for the Church as a DRE. I was an active volunteer, led communion services, preached Sunday liturgies in my former parish, wrote for an International homiletic publication, and formed a woman's liturgy group, among other things. No, I never was a woman religious! I did everything I could to give life to the Spirit of Vatican II. I now find great freedom away from Institutionalism." (71 yo female)

"I am beyond the institutional church now. Church politics, corruption, lack of transparency, child abuse efforts of cover up, failure to implement Vatican II mandate, the institutional turn to the extreme right and backwards trending, poorly prepared priests, bad homilies, and much more caused me and my family to leave the official church." (58 yo female)

"Until the Church accepts women and gay people as equals, unloads all of the excessive trappings, returns art to rightful owners or sells much of it for the benefit of the poor, and gets back to Jesus and what he taught us...well, until all that and more happens, I have no use for the current church. It is only the great figures of Catholicism—the mystics, a huge body of saints (although not all 'official' saints), it is only when LOVE is evident and the social teachings are out front that the church has meaning for me. I believe that God is present in each of us and we really don't need the Church per se...we need community and opportunities to share and serve." (71 yo female)

"Truth be known, I was never really happy with the

structural church and its position on women and exclusivity. The monks (of Glastonbury Abbey) are somewhat open, but cannot speak truth to power, and that has always been important to me." (64 yo female)

"This group (Illuminators) is way beyond the institutional church in some ways! It is post-denominational and is designed to set aside any connection to the "institutional church" and be a vehicle to discover deep inner spirituality, where the Divine actually resides!!! The only connection to early church would be the study of ancient illuminated texts and their purpose, design, colors, visual impact, etc." (female)

"I support gay rights, I'm a pacifist, and the environment and social justice are my two main concerns. The local Catholic Church is so hung up on Dogma that it seems to be ignoring the fact that we are rapidly destroying the planet...Today's church has become very ultra conservative, or should I say neoconservative. Pro-life has to be about more than the unborn...It was not anger that drew me away from Catholicism. I treasure much of what I've learned there, but it has become irrelevant in its smallness. Maintaining the institution and its hierarchy is its main concern." (female)

"The Roman Catholic institutional church is too big and cumbersome. In order to keep its power and stay in control it has been guilty of grave errors and unjust actions. One needs only to refer to Ratzinger's silencing of over one hundred distinguished scholars and Catholic disciples. This is a gave scandal, and that man leaves behind him a legacy that will earmark him as one of our most misguided, if not evil, of popes. Most faithful Catholics are innocently and naively unaware of this. When they are informed that Ratzinger has 'silenced' these Catholics, and it must be added—in a most shameful and cowardly way—they are stunned and shocked. Those who followed the "Way" inspired by Jesus of Nazareth witnessed to his life, teaching, and Paschal triumph, meeting in small communities. The tragedy of Constantine and his huge Roman basilicas speaks for itself in terms of the movement away from small communities." (male priest)

Small Numbers—How Important Is It to Keep your Community Small?

"Under 25 for ability to gather and understand one another in an intimate way and share goals, hopes, dreams. If it grows larger the group could divide and start another group."

"Keep it small...homes only have so much room."

"Small is good so everyone has the sense of community and caring about each other. Seems 10-20 is ideal since not everyone can make every liturgy."

"As such there is the opportunity to remain hidden and humble, without the trappings of a larger institution." (male)

"We really don't have issues [of leadership, mission, finance] since it is not an organized church. We meet, pray and share together and share a meal. We discuss ideas and hopefully grow together and reach out into the wider community with service." (female)

"Because it is a small group, everyone needs to participate actively to keep it going. I feel like I belong." (female)

"From a "therapeutic" perspective, small group format

possesses and exhibits a dynamic of 'family,' encouraging a bonding and interrelation between members of the group. Small community invites a shared spiritual experience that can be shared verbally and non-verbally, appreciated and validated by all members. This is a prayerful learning experience for all who participate!"

"I believe we have about fifty members. All are Roman Catholics who formerly belonged to various local parishes as well as those who had not affiliated with the church for many years. I hope we don't grow beyond one hundred members. It is difficult to get to know others on a personal basis if the group gets too large. I didn't know ninety-nine percent of the people at my old parish and then only a few on a close level. I have moved beyond the institutional church."

"We do not want to 'organize' or become an organization. We discussed it several times early on in our history and rejected it." (71 yo female)

"It is not important to keep it small but it is important to keep it intimate and honest."

"No more than 50. This way people know each other, it's like family." (female)

"Since we meet in homes and share food and materials, we have no expenses. It's great not to have to worry about money. We all contribute to charities and causes of our own choosing...not to church. Our bishop sent $50,000 to Connecticut to fight gay marriage." (71 yo female)

"We are an aging and small group (I am one of the 'young ones' at 60). Finances are very simple. We do not own a building, so give all that we can away. It would be good to do more." (60 yo female)

"I feel a need for spiritual conversation, and if the group gets too large it can become a lecture instead or can inhibit the sharing of the more timid members. I think a dozen would be the top number for this kind of group." (73 yo female)

"It is imperative to keep this group small for the purposes of communication, exchange of creative inspiration and phenomenology that occurs in the creation of art that has a deep mystic and Divine/spiritual source." (female)

"Our community is about 60 and out of the Roman Catholic tradition. I think it is extremely important to keep the community small. After 100, intimacy begins to be lost. I am no longer a part of the Roman Catholic Church. I believe the Roman Catholic church is not listening to the Spirit and is consumed with itself and not fostering in its ACTIONS the God life in each of us." (73 yo woman)

"It is important to keep it small because it is more intimate that way and we have a stronger commitment to one another as we develop and create history together. We've gone through many celebrations and tribulations together, births, deaths, marriages, divorces, all of it. We care about one another deeply." (70 yo female)

"Attendance is anywhere from 6-25 participants. Keeping the community small is very important. This allows for more intimate 'sharing'—as in 'shared homilies' (a tradition of ours), and conversation at the potlucks, as well as developing friendships and a sense of community. Currently we only manage to have two liturgies a month. Many who attend still are part of institutional parishes and involved there...We would be happy to be accepted as part of an existing RC community, use their facilities, but are not welcome in any around here. We like to describe ourselves as worshiping much as the Early Church did."

Brother Francis, I think you will agree with me that the wisdom expressed from the mouths of these current participants in small community must not be allowed to go to waste. There is much here that the larger church can learn from. I sense in these responses the deep alienation that the past two papacies have effected among many Catholics, don't you?

I am pleased that you are on board to support such communities and that you see they were part not only of Francis' hope for renewal of the church in his day but of the original Christ followers in the first century. Perhaps "success" and the marrying of church and empire in the fourth century set us on a detour.

7 THE SACRAMENT OF LIBERATION

Dear Pope Francis:

I recently read in the news that the beatification cause of Monsignor Romero has been "unblocked" since you became pope. It is well known that his beatification languished under the previous two popes who resisted him when he was alive and who denounced liberation theology.

How meaningful it would be to finally canonize Archbishop Oscar Romero who was martyred while celebrating a public Mass in El Salvador, killed by the military the day after he preached that "no soldier is obliged to obey an order that is contrary to the will of God." His murderers were supported by right wing landowners and a privileged oligarchy. His canonization would send a clear signal about the seriousness of the economic and political struggle that still goes on all around the world. In talking about the recent case of 1000 fatalities in the factory collapse in Bangladesh you referred to it as "slave labor" that "goes against God's will."

While the canonization of Romero would be deeply

meaningful, I also know that those who were close to him and his work have not been waiting on any papal noblesse to declare him a saint. They know the Church's tradition of how a martyr becomes a saint. Sister Dorothy and thousands of others who were tortured and martyred in Brazil, Chile and your own country Argentina, deserve to be recognized as saints. It is a sad thing that one of the reasons the Vatican silenced the holy Bishop Casigalida was that he called Romero, whom he knew well as a fellow bishop who was fighting a similar battle to his own in the Amazon, a "saint."

One Maryknoll missionary who served in Africa and South America told me that Pope John Paul II's obstruction of liberation theology and its communities resulted in "the death of thousands in Latin America." There were many who profited from this obstructionism, including the CIA, Wall Street and wealthy landowners in Latin America.

I believe your canonizing of Oscar Romero would be a very positive thing as it would signal an awareness of the immense sacrifices and holy courage and dedication to principles of justice and compassion that have marked so much of the community movements of Latin America in our lifetime. As I said earlier, Rome has not seen martyrs for untold centuries, but Latin America, in contrast, has been a killing ground for holy people standing up to unholy circumstances and unholy forces. Let us honor their witness and turn the page on the ignoring of these saintly contributions by so many in our time. In this way the Vatican might heed the teachings of Saint and Doctor of the Church, Hildegard of Bingen, who called Christ the chief cornerstone of the church and the laity the "living stones who adorn the church of God the most" and "embellish the church greatly" through their work for justice and compassion.

Perhaps we can now move beyond the rhetoric that has piled up around terms like "Marxism," "base communities," "Liberation Theology" and go back to the gospel message of liberation. As you once put it, "the option for the poor comes from the first centuries of Christianity. It is the Gospel itself." And you said that if you preached sermons from the first fathers of the church about the needs of the poor you would be called a "Maoist or Trotskyite."[11] Besides, you have spent much of your ministry working in slums.

Beyond rhetoric and politics lies the powerful Sacrament of Liberation, a sacrament that rose up in your continent as a living witness to the ever-present need to interfere with the injustice that obstructs the flow of grace that Life and God want all to experience. "I come that you may have life and have it in abundance." That is the Gospel invitation and removing the obstacles to this life, whether they are economic, ecological, political, gender or religious, is our task as followers of Jesus.

When I was silenced in 1990 for a year by then Cardinal Ratzinger as head of CDF, I went to Central and South America to see liberation theology and base communities up close. One place I visited was Bishop Casigalida's residence in the Amazon in Brazil which was, as you probably know, his parish. He put me up in his bed while he slept in another corner in the house, a house he shared with lay workers male and female. Over his bed was a charcoal drawing of him: I asked him, "What is the story behind that picture?" and he said a priest of his drew it while in prison and that he was tortured and killed in prison. So he kept it near to him, above his bed.

---

[11] Michael Warren, *et al*, "Pope Francis: Liberation Theology Priest Sees New Hope for Catholic Church," *Huffington Post Religion*, April 30, 2013.

MATTHEW FOX

The week I was visiting there was a retreat for about 250 church workers who were working with the indigenous peoples and others to defend the rainforest and the rainforest Indians. One evening they celebrated a Mass, together in a gymnasium, a very simple Mass with no grand gestures, parades of overly dressed clerics. At the end each person was invited to come up and light a candle and name three people they knew personally who had been tortured and murdered. Everyone in the room participated and lit a candle and named three names. Afterward one said to me: "The hard part was limiting it to three names as I know at least ten right off the top of my head."

I was thunderstruck by the courage of these ordinary people and reminded that we all have such courage within us when we truly believe in Gospel values and live them out. I am convinced that courage is today the number one evidence of the Spirit at work (as it was in the early church times). It is the grace of Christ, the teaching of Jesus and the lesson of Vatican II—to work and sacrifice for justice and compassion. How in heaven's name can the Vatican, except in the name of a sick and distorted religion, fight such a movement?

Such a church hierarchy has indeed chosen schism over the Gospel. I hope and pray you can bring the Church out of its schism and back to the Gospel. I hope and pray you can rebuild the Church—not alone but with many Christians who are working and have been working for some time both inside and outside church boundaries to see that the liberating and sacramental word of God is alive and spread where it is needed most.

It is of considerable interest to me that my Dominican (and your Italian) brother Thomas Aquinas says that redemption and liberation are the same thing. Redemption is not about our being saved from the wrath of God but from the wrath of our fellow humans and their institutions with their temptations to rapacity, greed and power over others. From such rapacity, greed and power, we all pray for redemption and liberation. You speak passionately about the "deformation of Christianity" that occurred when the papal states married "temporal and spiritual" powers. (1.226) This same deformation can happen whenever empires and religion collude.

Aquinas also teaches that the "primary" meaning of redemption is "preserving things in the good." What is a more fitting way to approach the great ecological challenges of our time than that? We must work to preserve the goodness of things, the health of the forests and rain forests, the animals, birds and fish the waters and rivers, the soil and the plants, and therefore the minds and bodies and hearts and spirits of the children who share this world and are to come after us.

Speaking of issues of liberation, it is essential to talk of women's rights. The growing awareness of the subjugation and oppression of women and the rights of women is a sign of our times. The Vatican Council urged us to heed the signs of our times. Wouldn't it be wonderful if the Vatican could join the people of God who are fighting for women's rights and to put an end to the horrible sex slavery and burdens of unneeded and unwanted pregnancies that burden women the world over? Up to now I have been disappointed by your rather off-the-cuff remarks about women in the church. It is pretty clear to me that you have not had the privilege—as I have had over the years—of sitting at the feet of honorable and committed women theologians to learn of their questions and profit from their scholarship. I think doing so will change some of your attitudes and religious thinking.

The attacks on the Leadership Conference of Women Religious (LCWR) is a scandal to a vast number of American Catholics who recognize women religious as people who have lived out and taught Gospel values and values of Vatican II, many in your continent. As one woman writer has put it, "Francis does not seem to understand that it is precisely because women religious regularly touch that wounded body of Christ that they have such rich theological imaginations and a longing to delve into the spiritual questions of our time."[12] Let us do away with silly talk about "radical feminism" and learn from our sisters.

The oppression of women in the name of religion ("man but not woman is made in the image and likeness of God" said Augustine, giving aid to this oppression with bad theology) is not just a Western or a Roman Catholic issue. The East too has had its share of misogyny toward women as is evidenced in a book I read recently called *Zen Women* which traces the struggles of Buddhist women to be leaders and cut through misogyny to found their own monasteries through the centuries.

This reality helps to realize that this "sign of our times" of the rise of women's rights and consciousness is a recent worldwide phenomenon and that it is not only western men (or western clerics) who felt deeply threatened by the suggestion of the rights of women. But things evolve—yes even doctrine evolves as John Henry Newman, newly canonized a saint, wrote about at length in the nineteenth century in his classic work, *The Development of Doctrine.* Doctrine evolves like everything else on earth and doctrines against birth control and against other women's

---

[12] Jamie Manson, "For LCWR, the more the papacy changes, the more it stays the same," *National Catholic Reporter*, May 9, 2013, http://ncronline.org.

needs and issues do evolve and must evolve.

Speaking of Buddhism and women's issues, I was moved a number of years ago when I was in the Dalai Lama's presence when he was asked: "What is your position on birth control?" He responded this way: "Our tradition has always been conservative about any form of life so we have traditionally been against birth control. But today, with the human population obviously driving out so many other species, we must change our position about birth control."

There is good precedent for a pope to confess anew the evolution of doctrines. One of Jesus' true breakthroughs was his teaching the equality of women. Unfortunately, the patriarchal church has turned its back on Jesus. Theologian Hans Kung sees the women issue as a key test of your willingness to truly rebuild the Church when he writes: "If Pope Francis tackles reforms, he will find he has the wide approval of people far beyond the Catholic Church. However, if he just lets things continue as they are, without clearing the logjam of reforms as now in the case of the Leadership Conference of Women Religious, then the call of "Time for outrage! Indignez-vous!" will ring out more and more in the Catholic Church, provoking reforms from the bottom up that will be implemented without the approval of the hierarchy and frequently even in spite of the hierarchy's attempts at circumvention. In the worst case...the Catholic Church will experience a new ice age instead of a spring and run the risk of dwindling into a barely relevant large sect."[13]

I hope your papacy will open new ground around these

---

[13] Hans Kung, "The Paradox of Pope Francis," *National Catholic Reporter*, May 27, 2013.

vital topics that concern us all.

A few years ago I had a dream that has grown in me ever since, and has had a lot to do with shaping my understanding of my vocation. In the dream the Spirit spoke with startling clarity: "There is nothing wrong with the human species today except one thing." Imagine that! There is only one thing wrong with us! Only one thing that needs curing and then we will all be alright. What is that one thing according to my dream? "You have forgotten the sense of the sacred."

I hope your papacy contributes mightily to that return of the sense of the sacred and I was pleased to read that theologian Leonardo Boff is encouraged that you respect for social action and for "what is sacred" can fix a church "in ruins" and work with people on the margins. As he put it, "Josef Ratzinger was against the cause of the poor, liberation theology. But this is from the last century. Now we are under a new Pope."[14]

What a Sacrament of Liberation reminds us is that liberation can't just be about a struggle for power, but must also be a struggle to bring the sacred back, to re-sacralize our relationships with the earth, our bodies, our children and generations to come, and to all the other creatures. Surely this is the Church's primary task today is it not? To evangelize, to remind us all, that we owe the earth so much and that we can, if we change our ways, render new life to our destructive ways of operating on the earth. Here lies redemption and liberation and the prophetic vocation we all share, the Via Transformativa. Here is where you, in the spirit of your namesake, as

---

[14] "Pope Francis: Liberation Theology Priest Sees New Hope for Catholic Church," *Huffington Post Religion*, April 30, 2013.

Bishop of Rome, can help engage the people to the works of justice and compassion. Already your shift toward the legacy of Francis has captured people's attention and you have the power to advance it greatly.

We can and need to move beyond politics alone to a sacramental approach to supporting human liberation around the world, honoring the poor, the under-employed, and those abused by abhorrent working conditions. It is clear you are already fighting on their behalf and including them in your public statements and prayers. I appreciate your perspective when you say: "Human rights are not just violated by terrorism, repression and murder...but also by the existence of extreme poverty and unjust economic structures that create huge inequalities." And when you name the structures as well: "The socioeconomic crisis and the resulting increase in poverty has its origin in policies inspired by forms of neo-liberalism that consider profit and the laws of the market as absolute parameters above the dignity of people or of peoples."[15]

I thank you for your recent "Address to the new non-resident Ambassadors to the Holy See" where you presented what you yourself called "an important" statement. There you take on the subjects of poverty, insecurity, fear and a "diminishing" of the joy of life and analyze the financial crisis of our times as a "profound human crisis" caused by the denial of the primacy of human beings and the elevation of "new idols." You speak the truth when you say "The worship of the golden calf of old has found a new and heartless image in the cult of money and the dictatorship of an economy which is

---

[15] "The new pope has a strong track record of speaking his mind, on everything from slavery to gay marriage," *The Guardian*, March 14, 2013. http://www.guardian.co.uk/world/2013/mar/14/new-pope-francis-in-his-own-words.

faceless and lacking any human goal." And an even deeper truth when you note how consumerism is the false religion wherein even people are "considered as consumer goods which can be used and thrown away" and "solidarity, which is the treasure of the poor, is often...opposed to the logic of finance and the economy." You decry the "absolute autonomy of markets and financial speculation" the lack of ethics while citing Saint John Chrysostom that "Not to share one's good with the poor is to rob them and to deprive them of life. It is not our goods that we possess, but theirs." You call for a "disinterested solidarity" and for a return to "person-centered ethics in the world of finance and economics" and a "balanced social order that is more humane."[16] Bravo! That is surely what the world needs and we thank you for giving a voice to it. Here in America Wall Street has overcome Main Street and the poor and unemployed suffer greatly.

Your language is something all can understand—hopefully even politicians—as when you speak of the "cult of money" and demand that "money has to serve, not rule!" Also when you speak of a "savage capitalism" that teaches "the logic of profit at any cost, of giving in order to get, of exploitation without thinking of people" and the results visible in the longer food kitchens and unemployment lines.[17] I and many appreciate your priorities when you make the point that "if investments in the banks fail, 'Oh, it's a tragedy.' But if people die of hunger or don't have food or health, nothing happens"

---

[16] "Address of Pope Francis to the New Non-Resident Ambassadors to the Holy See: Kyrgyzstan, Antigua and Barbuda, Luxembourg, and Botswana," May 16, 2013.

[17] "Pope criticizes 'savage capitalism' on visit to food kitchen," *Yahoo! News*, May 21, 2013, http://news.yahoo.com/pope-criticizes-savage-capitalism-visit-food-kitchen.

and that is reality constitutes "our crisis today."[18] I have just learned that you are planning an encyclical on Global Poverty. That is good news. You will have lots of support for that and I trust you will include the work of forward-thinking economists who are part of the growing majority who sense a need for an economics that works for everyone. Like your namesake, you are truly speaking to the needs and the hopes of the poor.

Let us recommit to the Biblical meaning of love, which includes justice and compassion. There can be no love without justice. We are all here to love and learn about love and to inculcate these values into economic and political structures that make them more possible.

In such a context as this, a truly universal and therefore catholic church would emerge again.

[18] Rachel Donadio, "Francis' Humility and Emphasis on the Poor Strike a New Tone at the Vatican," *The New York Times*, May 25, 2013.

8 TWELVE STEPS TO REBUILDING THE CHURCH

Dear Pope Francis:

I thank you for reading these letters and considering my ideas. I hope they might assist you in this great moment in your vocation, this amazing opportunity to contribute to the renewal of the Church, to undo the harm that the past decades of two schismatic papacies have wrought. I have faith in the people who are the church and I have faith in the Holy Spirit. I am confident you do also when you advise people that "if you want to know how to love Mary go to the People of God who teach it better" than theologians.[19] I hear you speaking of the *sensus fidelium* in this teaching of yours. I believe the Holy Spirit has put the Church through such a rough period over the past thirty-five years so that much of the apparatus and structures of the Church and the myths surrounding them could die off and a new life might rise and a new version

---

[19] "Pope: Open the door to faith," *Vatican Radio*, May 25, 2013.

of the Christ Path—one that more accurately reflects the message and person of Jesus might emerge.

We are on the same page when you observe that "if one looks at history, the religious forms of Catholicism have varied notably...If, throughout history, religion evolved so much, why wouldn't we think that in the future it will adjust to the culture of its time?" (1.226) Surely it is that kind of evolution we are all wrestling with today. What to keep and what to let go of?

Very early after your election you cited the phrase, "Repair my church in ruins." Those are strong words, a "church in ruins." You seem to have a sense of our times and how you have come along at a remarkable crossroads of time and history, not just church history, but more importantly planetary and human history. I beg you to keep that in mind in all of your decision-making. Remember you are not in this alone. I have sought to make some connections between your choice of St. Francis as your namesake and the deep needs of our present moment. We are in this together. No pope can save the Church alone, or should imagine he or she can do so. The people, who are the church, are already busy trying to. But it would be a great blessing if the Church's hierarchy, beginning with a refreshingly humble Bishop of Rome, would begin to assist rather than flagrantly obstruct these efforts.

You have chosen the hallowed name of Francis, a controversial choice of a name as I pointed out in my Introductory letter. One that sets the bar very high. People know Francis and they will be watching you because of that choice alone. They will be watching for signs, some of which I have listed in this book: Signs of commitment to the poor that is not just about personal pieties but includes real critique of what prevails today as economics and whether you will support those who offer alternatives for an economy that works for everyone (including all of creation); signs of commitment to a sustainable and ecological world where the human finds their humble place among the other species who also have rights and dignity and indeed carry the "Cosmic Christ" in them; signs of a new found balance of masculine and feminine, men and women, the Divine Feminine in tandem with the Sacred Masculine and acknowledgment of how religion itself has contributed to the subjugation of women; signs of invitation to creativity and adventure and joy that the young bring to the table; signs that ossified and insipid religion will not triumph over genuine practice, intellectual study and spiritual growth; signs that science and spirituality can and must work in consort; signs of authentic deep ecumenism and interfaith practice; and of course signs that you recognize the low state the current church finds itself in and that you are serious about implementing a clean-up and a cleaning out of the hen house that the Curia has become—a cleaning up of financial, sexual and theological messes.

Like Francis we will be expecting a great simplifying of the role of pope and Bishop of Rome. We will hope for a great Letting Go and Decentralization, a new level of trust (isn't that what faith is?) in the people who are the church and the Holy Spirit to lead them in fresh and vibrant manifestation of Jesus' teachings and person. And an invitation to an adventure of saving the planet we love and cherish and depend on, an adventure that beckons all humans and especially the younger generations.

Saint Hildegard of Bingen may have said it best when she said mother church proclaims: "I must receive and give birth." Her declaration of the deep role that creativity plays in community and church renewal is key. "Do you create or do you destroy?" is what the mystic and head of the United Nations, Dag Hammarskjold, asked over fifty years ago. I hope yours will be a papacy that creates. There are many at the grassroots world over, lay, priest, sisters, others who are working to see this reformation and indeed renaissance happen. We welcome your joining us.

To support what I believe is a commitment and value that we share, I offer in this final letter some directions and concrete ways in which you can, and in some instances already have proceeded to set in motion, some reforms of the Church and some directions for assisting the ethical and spiritual dimensions of rebuilding in the spirit of your namesake, Francis:

1. Invite married clergy back to ministry and tell the truth: Celibacy is optional.

It is my experience, Pope Francis, in knowing priests who have left to get married and those who have not that the loss to the church, i.e. the people, is more than just numbers of priests no longer in ministry. It is not just an issue of quantity. It is also an issue of quality. I believe most (not all) of the clergy who have remained are proven to be less flexible, less on the ball, less skilled in communication, less theologically curious and theologically read, frankly less mature than those who have left. There has been a decisive qualitative loss among the clergy as well as a quantitative loss.

The solution is obvious: Invite married clergy back, those who care to practice. This is not about putting up a lot of money to support their wives or children or grandchildren. It is about a part-time ministry; they have all proven they can survive without priestly stipends so they need not make any pecuniary demands. But many of them are ready and able to minister anew and to bring the wisdom they have learned from working and living in the world with them. They have much to offer. Why waste it in the name of a law of celibacy which is hardly a necessary norm for spreading the gospel since none of Jesus' followers were so sworn. Not even your suggested predecessor as Bishop of Rome, St Peter.

With a stroke of the pen you could upgrade the quality and quantity and intelligence and psychological health of the ordained priesthood by simply stating the obvious: Celibacy is a special chrism especially for monks but it is not a requirement for the priesthood or church leadership. Period.

2. Cease the (sick) preoccupation with sexual ethics and pelvic morality.

The Church's record on sexual ethics seems, to so many, as all talk and no action. Whether one is talking of pre-marital sex, birth control, homosexuality, condoms, AIDS, population explosion, pedophilia, celibacy, divorce and remarriage, women's rights or abortion—the actions of so many priests and prelates belie the constant messaging of No! No! No! It seems to me, as it seemed to the Celtic poet I cited early in this book, that the hierarchy protesteth too much and in many instances (for example the Cardinal of Scotland referred to earlier) practiceth too little.

What is the medicine for this preoccupation with pelvic morality? Silence. Yes, I think about fifteen years of silence is in order from the institutional church. Just shut up about sex. People are mature and adult enough to figure out values about responsible sexuality—and that is what is at stake here— without the constant interventions and often zealous ranting about sexual issues from a so-called celibate hierarchy.

This silence would allow clerics and others to focus on other and more pressing moral issues of our time such as the shortage of work, the oppression of women and young people, and the demise of our ecosystems and numerous species that are going extinct because of harmful ways of living on the earth and militarism and how it robs us of money that can be used for important and needed causes including good education and relief of the misery of the poor. Again, a simple teaching about sexuality should be enough for now: Practice responsible sex. For the rest, let silence reign.

A number of years ago when Pope John Paul II was visiting the United States and many Catholics were flocking to his outdoor Mass in the state of Kansas, a reporter interviewed a fifteen old boy who was in the crowd and eagerly awaiting the pope's arrival. The reporter reminded him that the pope was against birth control and condoms. The fifteen year old responded by saying: "What? That's impossible! What about AIDS? What about the population explosion around the world?" This is the *sensus fidelium* talking. When a fifteen year old is smarter about sexual morality than a pope, it is indeed time for popes to be silent and listen deeply.

3. Go ahead and canonize Oscar Romero and all those who have fought and died for justice in South America.

My great Dominican brother Meister Eckhart once asked: "Who is a good person?" And he answered his question this way: "A good person is one who praises good people." Surely Pope Francis you are eager to praise the courage and Gospel witness to justice and compassion that your fellow Latin American theologians and communities have borne witness to, are you not? Surely you are proud of these people—and their Christ-like practices on behalf of the poor, and the soil and rainforests on which all life depends? And their courage in standing up to address power directly? How about the blood they shed in the name of justice? Not only Oscar Romero and Sister Dorothy Stang who stood up to be counted as "presente," but also your four Jesuit brothers slaughtered in El Salvador along with their housekeeper and her daughter? The thousands tortured under Pinochet because they stood for justice and democracy? Great bishops like Helder Camera and Bishop Casigalida and Cardinal Arns who dared to stand up to the military in Brazil even while their priests, sisters and lay people were being tortured to death in prison?

We have been blessed by knowing of these many good persons in our lifetime, so many tested and tried on the South American continent, your homeland. Surely they are deserving of praise and emulation for carrying on their battles into the twenty-first century. It is significant that those who have led the way have done so in the so-called "third world" and in the southern hemisphere which for so long was a place of colonial abuse and profiteering. In your new position as pope you are free to bring attention to the rivers of blood spent and the values that inspired these sacrifices. The blood of our martyrs could launch a new Christianity—a Christ Path rather than an imperial church.

4.   While you are praising these great souls, it would be a significant gesture to remove some of the gold that now adorns many churches in Rome and was seized from the indigenous peoples of South America, often under the banner of slavery and deportations.

It seems only just and right to return this gold to the descendants of these people, those who still inhabit the South American continent. I think Francis would approve—as you say, he "was the poor man who wanted a poor church." (10.17) A gesture like this seems in tune with your values of simplicity and sensitivity to the poor that you have borne witness to for years. (In addition, it helps to highlight and remind people of the price indigenous peoples have paid in the past for imperial European actions and their impact on American history.)

I and many others appreciate your gesture to refuse to move into papal palaces. But while you are doing such resisting, it might also be fitting to have someone look into the basement of the Vatican museum for all the treasures of sculpture and paintings that are amassed there and to sell these items and see to it that every euro acquired goes into a fund to support the poorest of the poor in Africa, Latin America and southeast Asia. Perhaps the mosaics, paintings and sculpture that still grace the Vatican museum itself could continue to be left there in hopes that the tourists and pilgrims who pay to see them might also see their money used to alleviate hunger and combat disease around the world.

5. I think it is important to call to justice the radical sects inside the Church that have made such headway during the past two papacies. I speak of course of Opus Dei, Communion and Liberation, Legion of Christ, Focolare and more.

I was struck when I heard in an interview with your sister that the reason your ancestors left Italy to migrate to Argentina was to escape fascism. Good for them! Surely your experience growing up in Argentina was not devoid of up-close experience with fascism. After all, Argentina became a dumping ground for Nazis and Italian fascists after World War II and surely your military junta that ruled with intimidation and murders and torture for seven years was fascist to the core. Thank God for the grandmothers who protested daily over so many years in order that the truth of the "disappeared" would be known.

Susan Sontag, a very well respected cultural critic in the United States, defined fascism as "institutionalized violence." The scandal of priestly pedophilia and above all its cover up by cardinals and even popes certainly qualifies as institutionalized violence as does violence toward thinkers (called "theologians") and to people who would have profited by the continued development of theology. There is also the institutional violence toward priests who marry, unless of course you are a married Anglican priest and can demonstrate that you 1) are a deep sexist and therefore rabidly committed to no women priests ever and 2) are a committed homophobe, equally zealous about keeping gays out of the clergy (even though from the very beginning, there have always been gay clergy). The violence is not just against the priests as individuals but against all those who might have profited spiritually from having a healthy priest with whom to communicate and relate.

There is institutionalized violence toward homosexuals and toward women.

I recognize fascism as a world view that is totally patriarchal, top-down, hierarchical, that honors power-over and elevates a teaching of God as a punitive father putting fear and obedience forward as primary virtues in contrast to creativity or solidarity. It is the ultimate triumph of patriarchal domination over partner relationships. I hear you speaking to these issues at the pastoral level when you say that too often "protocol" or "pastoral customs" and "closed doors" take precedence in parishes and that "we are many times controllers of faith, instead of becoming facilitators of the faith of the people." You call for "open doors!" and many are the Christians who want to hear that message.[20]

We North Americans, for all our faults, nevertheless know something about fascism. We stood up (along with many others) two generations ago to fight it. Millions lost their lives or their limbs in doing so. Fascism is not an abstraction to us. It is part of history and the shadow of humankind. In my own family one uncle was in the army and helped to liberate France as well as Dachau and another fought in the Pacific theater in such atrocious battles as Iwo Jima and Guadalcanal as a marine. They both saw lots of death and destruction as young men and put their lives on the line battling fascism.

Surely a church claiming to speak in the name of Jesus' message of justice and compassion ought to ferret out fascism both within its organization and beyond. Pinochet, Father Maciel, Jose Escriva, Cardinal Sodano, and all champions of fascism need to be called out. They, and not theologians of liberation or of Creation Spirituality, are the ones who set the Church on a wayward path for decades. It is my observation that more Catholics have left the Church for its radical right turn in politics than for any other reason.

6.   While you are at it, it is necessary to clean up the canonization process.

This process was besmirched under the two previous papacies when they threw out the devil's advocate, which for centuries had been integral. How else could Jose Escriva, founder of Opus Dei and a card carrying fascist who actually plotted to get himself canonized,[21] who

---

[20] Ibid.

[21] Michael Walsh, *Opus Dei: An Investigation into the Secret Society*

admired Hitler, who supported the fascist dictator Franco with members of his order in his cabinet, who fought Vatican II tooth and nail, who screamed at women and called them "whores" if his eggs were not cooked right or the altar cloths were less than perfect, ever be declared a saint? He was rushed into sainthood faster than anyone in history and we are all the worse for it as Opus Dei hierarchy now prevail on many continents. The only way this could happen is by forbidding people who knew him well, such as his secretary of seven years, to testify during the canonization process. (13.106-124)

It is not only the devil's advocate that needs to be addressed in the canonization scandals but the money element as well. How much did the wealth of Opus Dei influence the canonization of Escriva? Is saintliness for sale these days in the Curia? There also seems to be a sort of closed circle of hagiography in the Curia these days as one suspects they are busy canonizing one another.

7. About the Vatican Bank. Close it.

Why does the Bishop of Rome need his own bank? Whom is it truly serving? We all know the bountiful scandals that have been associated with that bank for a long, long time. Things were so sordid just a year ago that the Italian government refused to accept Vatican credit cards while they were investigating what we have been hearing about for generations—money laundering, drug cartel cash, and more. The world knows about the banker Roberto Calvi whose body was found hanging from a bridge in London and who was deeply involved with both Opus Dei and the temporary rescue of the Vatican bank and how the Vatican bank helped to finance despotic

Struggling for Power within the Roman Catholic Church (San Francisco: HarperSanFrancisco, 1992), p. 195.

regimes in Latin America that persecuted priests, nuns and lay workers. And how the Vatican bank was run by a mobster, Michele Sindona who was eventually arrested and imprisoned in the United States where he was murdered in jail. (13. 115, 167f) We also know that Pope John Paul I was intent on cleaning up the sordid state of the Vatican bank but died a sudden death before he could do so. Enough is enough! Cut the Gordian knot. Get the Church out of the banking business once and for all.

8. About the Congregation of the Doctrine of Faith and the New Inquisition. End it.

I was struck in your dialog with Rabbi Skorka who said that a sign of a false prophet is absolute certitude and that God is dynamic and changes His mind and that we cannot talk of God's messages in absolute terms but that a truly religious leader is humble. You reply that "the bad leader is the one who is self-assured, and stubborn [and] excessively normative because of his self-assurance." You say, "when someone is self-sufficient, when he has all the answers to every question, it is proof that God is not with him. Self-sufficiency is evident in every false prophet, in the misguided religious leaders that use religion for their own ego. It is the stance of religious hypocrites because they speak about God, who is above all things, but they do not put into practice His commands." (1.32f)

I appreciate your comments because for me they help to explain why we do not need inquisitors in this day and age. The Vatican Council said as much when it created an entire decree on "Declaration of Religious Freedom" and when it encouraged lively and spirited debate among theologians. Third rate theologians, most of whom have never published a book in their life, hiding out in the old and dank offices of the "Sacred Inquisition" propounding about what is and is not orthodox is a bad joke from the past. Let them find honest work. Let that task of the CDF, which has been ignored for decades, be the chasing down of wayward clergy who are pedophile priests, as well as those hierarchy who cover up for them—and let it proceed as a stand-alone agency. Let it be run by laymen and laywomen, so that ecclesial favors are not part of the serious criminal investigations that are sure to follow.

Do not just end the Inquisition which has driven many theologians and pastoral leaders into poverty, psychological breakdowns and even heart attacks over the past two papacies, encourage thinking! Bring theology back. If it is true, as indicated by the story I told earlier from a professor at my alma mater that the two recent popes "killed all theology in Europe," then maybe this has something to do with the collapse of religion in Europe: the colossal and deliberate dumbing down of the Church. Surely as a Jesuit with a proud intellectual tradition you do not believe in inquisitions, do you? It truly is an embarrassment in our times that the Church traffics in unprofessional and insulting attacks on thinkers. A dumbed down church is an empty church.

9. You need to address the appointment of hierarchical leadership as well.

I was pleased to hear of the new appointee as bishop in my diocese of Oakland recently, a Jesuit who seems not to have climbed the clerical ladder but appears to be someone who genuinely cares about people.

The coup d'eglise that we have suffered through for the past two papacies has been cemented by the complete centralization of everything—liturgical practice, magisterial teaching including spreading fear among theologians, support of so-called lay orders that answer only to Rome, the disempowerment of laity and the disempowerment of national bishop councils and surely the appointment of bishops and cardinals. Now it is true that since all such appointments are schismatic none of the appointees need be heeded by the people who are the church. But the problem and the precedent remain: The Vatican council tried to decentralize appointments and the Curia took them back by their grand scheme of centralization (and in the process got an absurd number of their own to be named cardinals). Return leadership roles to those who know the leaders themselves, those who live, work and observe them in their own respective dioceses around the world.

I encourage you to write many of these cardinals and bishops with your very words which are so applicable to them when you say: "The teacher who is so arrogant as to make decisions for the disciple is not a good priest, he's a good dictator, an eraser of the religious personalities of others...this kind of religiosity, so rigid, wraps itself in doctrines that pretend to provide justifications, but in reality they deny liberty and don't allow people to grow."[22]

Of course there is something more profound at work here as well. Let the word go out to all those who have chosen blind obedience to theological depth that it is time to learn the wonderful findings in today's Biblical scholarship and in the revelations from today's science about the universe we live in. Let them find the mystic and the prophet in themselves and encourage it in others. Insist that they grow up and quit obsessing about sexual morality. Let them learn Francis' and Hildegard's and Aquinas' and Jesus' tradition of wisdom or Creation Spirituality.

---

[22] Michael Warren, "Pope Francis, in his own words, on the issues," *loc cit*.

It is time to re-train all those anointed during the schismatic times. Happily, I offer my services to create programs that can retrain schismatic clergy just as we were successful in retraining engineers and many other adults. It is also time to bring some gender balance into the big picture. Already many women hold respectable theological credentials. And, as we discussed above, the authentic leadership is a lay leadership when all is said and done and many Christian lay leaders (including artists and others) are just waiting to be invited to the table.

10. Recharge deep ecumenism.

Thankfully, you seem genuinely sensitive to the fact that the Holy Spirit "blows where it will" and surely breathes both through other Christian traditions both Eastern and Western as well as through Judaism, Buddhism, Hinduism, Islam and indigenous traditions. Your record on dialoging with persons of other faith traditions is a positive one. Your symbolic action of washing a Muslim woman's feet in prison on Holy Thursday did not go unnoticed in the Muslim community as evidenced by an appreciative article in the *Huffington Post* by an ecumenical and activist Muslim. In addition, your meeting with ecumenical church leaders and having your chair on the ground and not elevated was another gesture of sensitivity to the worth of other traditions. I hope this attitude prevails and advances in your papacy.

Your recent call for finding common ground with atheists is also encouraging when you said that if people "just do good, we'll find a meeting point." Amen to that![23]

---

[23] "Just do good, and we'll find a meeting point, says Francis in marked departure from Benedict's line on non-Catholics," *The Guardian*, May 22, 2013.

Given the crisis of the survival of our species and of the planet itself that we all face today, surely it is time to move beyond tribalism and sectarianism and to find those areas we can work on together as well as pray and celebrate together. Surely we can all acknowledge that the sacredness of creation is at the heart of all of our faith traditions as is calming our reptilian brains (thus meditation) and honoring our holy imaginations and practicing compassion (which includes justice). The Dalai Lama has said, "we can do away with all religion but we cannot do away with compassion. Compassion is my religion." Well, compassion was also at the heart of Jesus' religion (see Lk 6:36: "Be you compassionate as your Father in heaven is compassionate").[24]

Another issue we can all agree on is that greed and avarice are not virtues—no matter how loudly Wall Street preaches otherwise and no matter how powerfully they line up forces of international corporate megaliths to carry out their institutionalized greed. What would St Francis say about the economic imbalance of our times? Surely it is time that all the world religions gather to lay out, with the help of many economists who have been working on this for years, an economics that works for everyone.[25] And by everyone we must include the non-two-legged creatures, the forests and oceans and beasts and birds that are also subject to the choices humans make which so impact their survival as well as our own.

Wouldn't it be fitting and a hopeful sign for you and the Dalai Lama to sit down and dialog and put the word

---

[24] I treat 17 themes that all faith traditions share in my book, *One River, Many Wells: Wisdom Springing from Global Faiths.*

[25] I have in mind, for example, the valuable work of David Korten in such books as *Agenda for a New Economy: From Phantom Wealth to Real Wealth* and *When Corporations Rule the World.*

out together to the whole world of the shared directions of eco-justice and economic justice that compassion requires and our sustainability as a species requires? It is time to get the train of ecumenism running again; it has been derailed for over thirty years. The Second Vatican Council both urged it and practiced it.

11. Support small communities and women's rights inside and outside the Church and end the current inquisition aimed at women religious in the United States.

In my sixth letter I shared with you some of the deep wisdom from experimental small communities. Any time like ours which requires a "return to the sources" requires a support of such small communities and I hope you continue to offer it.

This month marks the first year anniversary of the Vatican Congregation of the Doctrine of Faith's efforts to demean the wonderful witness of Catholic Sisters in the United States under their chosen leadership conference known as the LCWR. One hopes that your papacy will end this ill-chosen effort to intimidate these generous and Gospel-driven sisters (of which Sister Dorothy Stang was one) who have been living out the values and principles of Vatican II.

Let us apply Meister Eckhart's words that I cited earlier, that "a good person praises good people." The Vatican should be PRAISING these sisters who are living out Gospel values and the values of Vatican II, including those of courage and support of the poor. Investigating these sisters is a scandal to all who know them and their devoted work over the years. The Vatican needs to educate itself on the various ministries that women performed in the earliest church and wake up to the needs of today and the gifts women bring to the table in our time.

12. Unleash a tsunami of creativity including forms of worship.

Today artists of all kinds—street artists, performing artists, musicians, poets, rappers, b-boys, architects and others—are just waiting to be invited to participate in bringing imagination and joy and the new creation story from science into our worship and into rituals of all kinds. I have spoken earlier of the draw that our Cosmic Masses have had for artists of many stripes. With so much unemployment around the world today, we should be encouraging artists to bring their gifts of aliveness and joy into the realm of community celebration and spiritual practice. In the past the Church has a fairly decent record of encouraging art and inspiring artists. The human species to survive needs an explosion of creativity and imagination in order to remake the way we live on the earth. Artists can assist in this global renaissance. Many can be put to good work in the process.[26] Can the Church lead instead of just wait passively or condemn?

When Emperor Constantine became a Christian in the fourth century he turned over many pagan temples that were vast in size (for example, the Pantheon in Rome) to the Christians. It was then that the Church started to dress the clergy up in fancy clothes and tall miters and hats—so that they could be seen and noticed in so vast and theatrical a setting. While this footnote from history helps to explain how bishops and cardinals and others got into such elaborate finery for Liturgy, it does not give a

---

[26] I treat this topic as part of *The Reinvention of Work* in my book by that title.

theological reason for it. It cannot do so in fact. It is about theater and being seen and heard. With microphones and the rest today, such elaborate costuming can and ought to be seriously curtailed.

I am pleased to see in you, Pope Francis, sensitivity to this issue. The days of arguing whether the pope is wearing Gucci shoes or Prada sunglasses hopefully are behind us. Simplification and downsizing are clearly in order. We are no longer trying to rival the entertainment of the imperial court vestment by vestment and spectacle by spectacle. Liturgy is the work of the people—not of one person elevated above the rest of us in imperial fashion. Please continue your efforts to simplify the wardrobe and ceremonies that smack of the Constantinian imperial church and not at all of the church of the people.

The creativity tsunami I refer to carries us far beyond ritual of course into areas of reinventing economics, politics, media, education and religion. In your dialogs with Rabbi Skorka I was pleased to hear you speak of "an extremely creative justice" that "invents things: education, social progress, care and attention, relief," as well as culture itself. (1.22f)

To this I say: Amen. Can the organized church contribute to all of this? One would hope so.

Fraternally and Godspeed,

Matthew Fox, oops (once of the order of preachers)

BIBLIOGRAPHY

1.   Jorge Mario Bergoglio and Abraham Skorka, *On Heaven and Earth* (New York: Image, 2013).

1a.   Jason Berry and Gerald Renner, *Vows of Silence: The Abuse of Power in the Papacy of John Paul II* (New York: Free Press, 2004).

2.   Thomas Berry, *The Great Work: Our Way into the Future* (New York: Bell Tower, 1999).

3.   Leonardo Boff, *Saint Francis: A Model for Human Liberation* (New York: Crossroad, 1984).

4.   Adam Bucko and Matthew Fox, *Occupy Spirituality: A Radical Vision for a New Generation* (Berkeley, Ca: North Atlantic Books, 2013).

5.   Pierre Teilhard de Chardin, *The Divine Milieu* (New York: Harper & Row, 1960).

6.   Pierre Teilhard de Chardin, *The Heart of Matter* (New York: Harcourt Brace Jovanovich, 1978).

7.   Pierre Teilhard de Chardin, *Human Energy* (New York: Harcourt Brace Jovanovich, 1969).

8.   Pierre Teilhard de Chardin, *Hymn of the Universe* (New York: Harper & Row, 1965).

9.   M. D. Chenu, *Nature, Man and Society in the Twelfth Century* (Chicago: University of Chicago Press, 1968).

10.   Julie Schwietert Collazo and Lisa Rogak, eds, *Pope Francis in His Own Words* (Novato, Ca: New World

Library, 2013).

11.   Matthew Fox, *Hildegard of Bingen, A Saint for Our Times: Unleashing Her Power in the 21st Century* (Vancouver: Namaste, 2012).

12.   Matthew Fox, *A New Reformation* (Rochester, Vt.: Inner Traditions, 2006).

13.   Matthew Fox, *The Pope's War: How Ratzinger's Secret Crusade Imperiled the Church and How It Can Be Saved* (New York: Sterling Ethos, 2011).

14.   Abraham Joshua Heschel, *God in Search of Man: A Philosophy of Judaism* (New York: Farrar, Straus, and Cudahy, 1955).

ABOUT THE AUTHOR

Matthew Fox holds a Ph.D. in spirituality, summa cum laude, from the Institut Catholique de Paris. His long career of creating alternative pedagogies for teaching a mystical and prophetic spirituality includes founding the Institute of Culture and Creation Spirituality, which was shut down after 19 years under pressure from then-Cardinal Ratzinger whose pursuit of him led to Fox's "silencing" in 1989 and ultimate expulsion from the Dominican Order in 1993. He started the University of Creation Spirituality and has been active as a priest in the Anglican community since being expelled from the Dominicans, teaching and working with youth to create a more just and compassionate world—one in keeping with spirit of St. Francis. His 31 books have received numerous awards and have been translated into 49 languages. Learn more at www.matthewfox.org.

Books by Matthew Fox

Occupy Christianity: A Radical Vision for a New Generation—with Adam Bucko

Hildegard of Bingen: A Saint for Our Times

The Pope's War: Why Ratzinger's Secret Crusade Has Imperiled the Church and How It Can Be Saved

Christian Mystics: 365 Readings and Meditations

The Hidden Spirituality of Men: Ten Metaphors to Awaken the Sacred Masculine

The A.W.E. Project: Reinventing Education, Reinventing the Human

A New Reformation: Creation Spirituality & the Transformation of Christianity

Creativity: Where the Divine and the Human Meet

Prayer: A Radical Response to Life (formerly *On Becoming a Musical, Mystical Bear*)

One River, Many Wells: Wisdom Springing From Global Faiths

Sins of the Spirit, Blessings of the Flesh: Lessons for Transforming Evil in Soul and Society

The Physics of Angels – with biologist Rupert Sheldrake

Natural Grace – with biologist Rupert Sheldrake

Passion for Creation: The Earth-Honoring Spirituality of Meister Eckhart (formerly *Breakthrough*)

Wrestling With the Prophets: Essays on Creation Spirituality and Everyday Life

The Reinvention of Work: A New Vision of Livelihood For Our Time

Sheer Joy: Conversations with Thomas Aquinas on Creation Spirituality

Creation Spirituality: Liberating Gifts for the Peoples of the Earth

The Coming of the Cosmic Christ: The Healing of Mother Earth and The Birth of a Global Renaissance

Illuminations of Hildegard of Bingen

Original Blessing: A Primer in Creation Spirituality

Meditations with Meister Eckhart

A Spirituality Named Compassion

Confessions: The Making of a Post-Denominational Priest

Hildegard of Bingen's Book of Divine Works, Songs & Letters

Whee! We, Wee All the Way Home: A Guide to Sensual, Prophetic Spirituality

Religion USA: Religion and Culture by way of TIME Magazine

Manifesto for a Global Civilization--with Brian Swimme

Passion for Creation: Meister Eckhart's Creation Spirituality

In the Beginning There Was Joy (children's book, illustrated)

Western Spirituality: Historical Roots, Ecumenical Routes (editor)

All media and rights inquiries to:
LevelFiveMedia, LLC
4 W. South Orange Avenue
Third Floor
South Orange, NJ 07079 USA
LevelFiveMedia@aol.com

CPSIA information can be obtained at www.ICGtesting.com
Printed in the USA
LVOW12s1429050214

372484LV00015B/340/P